Yu-Gi-Oh! Holiday Gifting Mastery

Yu-Gi-Oh! Holiday Gifting Mastery

Matthew Petchinsky

Yu-Gi-Oh! Holiday Gifting Mastery: The Ultimate Guide for Fans and Newcomers Alike

By: Matthew Petchinsky

Introduction: The World of Yu-Gi-Oh!

The world of *Yu-Gi-Oh!* is a vibrant, thrilling universe that spans across anime, manga, video games, and perhaps most notably, its highly popular trading card game (TCG). Since its debut in the late 1990s, *Yu-Gi-Oh!* has evolved into one of the most beloved and competitive card games worldwide, amassing millions of fans and collectors. What began as a simple concept of "dueling" between characters in a manga series by Kazuki Takahashi has now grown into a global phenomenon, with intricate strategies, regional and world tournaments, and a constantly evolving set of cards. With over 10,000 unique cards in existence, the *Yu-Gi-Oh!* TCG offers endless possibilities for customization, deck building, and gameplay innovation.

Popularity of the Yu-Gi-Oh! Card Game: *Yu-Gi-Oh!* is more than just a card game; it's a cultural phenomenon that has captivated players of all ages. The game's popularity stems from its rich lore, complex gameplay mechanics, and the strong sense of community it fosters among its players. The core appeal lies in the strategy behind every duel—players must outwit and outmaneuver their opponents using a combination of monsters, spells, and traps, each with their own unique abilities and interactions. The diversity in deck-building options means no two duels are alike, allowing for constant evolution and creativity in playstyle.

Tournaments, local game shops, and online communities thrive on the competitive aspect of *Yu-Gi-Oh!*, with new expansions and booster packs regularly released to keep the game fresh and dynamic. Whether players are serious competitors who enter regional championships or casual fans who enjoy a friendly match at home, *Yu-Gi-Oh!* offers something for everyone. The game's sustained popularity can also be attributed to its nostalgic value; many who watched the original anime or played the early versions of the game as children continue to participate as adults.

Why Yu-Gi-Oh! Makes a Fantastic Gift: Given the game's immense popularity and the wide variety of cards, accessories, and themed merchandise available, *Yu-Gi-Oh!* makes an exceptional gift for fans of the franchise. Whether you're gifting a seasoned player or someone new to the world of dueling, there is no shortage of exciting options to choose from, including booster packs, starter decks, exclusive collector's items, and card accessories like sleeves and binders. Not only are these gifts fun and interactive, but they also allow players to expand their collections and improve their gameplay experience.

For collectors, limited-edition cards, commemorative sets, and high-quality playmats or card sleeves can be especially meaningful. For players, a well-thought-out booster box or structured deck can help them refine their skills or explore new strategies. Even for those who enjoy the franchise casually through the anime or video games, *Yu-Gi-Oh!* memorabilia such as figurines, apparel, or themed games can serve as a great introduction to the deeper world of the card game.

How to Select the Perfect Yu-Gi-Oh! Gift: If you're not familiar with the game but want to give the perfect *Yu-Gi-Oh!* gift, don't worry! Selecting the right item largely depends on the recipient's level of involvement and specific interests within the franchise.

- **For beginners or younger fans**, starter decks are a fantastic choice. These pre-built decks offer a balanced introduction to the game's core mechanics and are an excellent gateway for those just beginning to explore the world of *Yu-Gi-Oh!*.
- **For intermediate players** who are building their own decks but may not have a large card collection yet, booster packs or tins are ideal. These contain a variety of random cards that can help strengthen their decks and give them access to rare or powerful cards. Alternatively, a card binder for organization or a deck box for storing their cards can be useful.

- **For advanced players or collectors**, focus on rarer or more exclusive items like special edition cards, high-end card sleeves, or official playmats. These players will appreciate the thoughtfulness behind gifts that help them enhance their gameplay or collection. Limited-edition box sets, tournament kits, or rare holographic cards are always sure to impress.
- **For fans of the anime or manga** who may not play the card game competitively, you can explore merchandise outside of the TCG. Action figures, DVDs, or clothing featuring favorite characters or iconic monsters from the series, such as the Blue-Eyes White Dragon or Dark Magician, can be a great way to tap into their love for the franchise.

The beauty of *Yu-Gi-Oh!* as a gift is that there is truly something for everyone. With a little insight into the recipient's level of interest and style of play, you can find the perfect gift that will add excitement, joy, and value to their *Yu-Gi-Oh!* experience. Whether your recipient is a hardcore duelist or just enjoys the nostalgia, the world of *Yu-Gi-Oh!* offers an endless array of options to make your gift truly special.

Chapter 1: Understanding the Yu-Gi-Oh! Card Game

The *Yu-Gi-Oh!* Trading Card Game (TCG) is a strategic and dynamic game where players, called "duelists," compete using specially designed decks of cards. These cards represent powerful monsters, spells, and traps that duelists use to outwit their opponents. The game, initially inspired by the manga and anime series created by Kazuki Takahashi, has developed into one of the most beloved and competitive trading card games in the world. For those new to *Yu-Gi-Oh!*, understanding its mechanics, terminology, and the types of cards available is crucial to appreciating the depth of the game and making informed gift decisions.

Overview of the Game

The goal of a *Yu-Gi-Oh!* duel is simple: reduce your opponent's Life Points (LP) to zero before they do the same to you. Each player begins with 8,000 Life Points and a deck of at least 40 cards. Players take turns drawing and playing cards to summon monsters, activate powerful spells, or set traps to counter their opponent's moves. Victory often requires a combination of strategy, timing, and deck synergy.

While the premise may seem straightforward, the game's complexity emerges through the interaction of various card effects, timing, and resource management. *Yu-Gi-Oh!* is a fast-paced game where duelists must balance offense and defense, manage limited resources, and anticipate their opponent's next move. This mixture of strategy and unpredictability makes every duel unique.

Terminology: The Language of Dueling

To understand *Yu-Gi-Oh!* fully, it's essential to grasp some basic terminology frequently used in the game:

- **Duel**: A match between two players, each aiming to reduce the opponent's Life Points to zero.
- **Deck**: A set of at least 40 cards that a duelist uses in a duel. Decks are custom-built by players to suit their playstyle and strategy.
- **Draw Phase**: The first phase of a player's turn, where they draw a card from their deck.
- **Main Phase**: The part of the turn where players can summon monsters, activate spells, or set traps.
- **Battle Phase**: The phase in which a player attacks with their monsters to deal damage to their opponent or their opponent's monsters.
- **End Phase**: The final part of a turn, when effects that last until the end of the turn resolve and the next player takes over.
- **Field**: The area where cards are played during a duel, including zones for monsters, spells, traps, and the graveyard (discard pile).
- **Chain**: A game mechanic that describes the stacking of card effects in response to each other. Chains allow players to react to their opponent's moves in a specific sequence.

Types of Cards

At the heart of *Yu-Gi-Oh!* are the three main types of cards: Monster Cards, Spell Cards, and Trap Cards. Each card type plays a different role in the game, and understanding these roles is essential for any duelist.

1. **Monster Cards**: Monster cards represent the creatures and warriors duelists summon to fight on their behalf. Monsters are the backbone of most duels, and understanding their mechanics is crucial to building a successful strategy.
   - **Normal Monsters**: These monsters have no special abilities beyond their raw attack and defense stats. They are represented by yellow backgrounds and are often used as straightforward attackers or defenders.
   - **Effect Monsters**: These monsters possess special abilities that can turn the tide of a duel. Their effects can range from destroying opponent's cards to summoning other monsters. They are essential in modern decks.
   - **Fusion, Synchro, Xyz, and Link Monsters**: These monsters are summoned from the Extra Deck using special summoning methods. Each of these subtypes requires specific conditions to be met in order to summon them, adding layers of strategy to deck-building and gameplay.
     - **Fusion Monsters**: Summoned by combining monsters with a Fusion Spell Card.
     - **Synchro Monsters**: Summoned by using a Tuner monster and other monsters with levels that add up to match the Synchro Monster's level.
     - **Xyz Monsters**: Summoned by overlaying two or more monsters of the same level. These monsters use "Rank" instead of level.
     - **Link Monsters**: Summoned by using a number of monsters, depending on their Link Rating, and have no DEF stat or levels.

- **Tribute Summon**: Some monsters require a "tribute," meaning you must sacrifice other monsters already on the field to summon them, especially for higher-level monsters.

2. **Spell Cards**: Spell cards (formerly called Magic cards) provide powerful, one-time or continuous effects that can support monsters, weaken the opponent, or manipulate the state of the game. Spells can only be activated during a player's turn unless otherwise stated.

   - **Normal Spells**: These can be activated only once during a turn and are then sent to the graveyard.
   - **Continuous Spells**: These stay on the field after activation, continuously providing their effects until they are destroyed.
   - **Equip Spells**: Attach to a specific monster, enhancing its power or abilities.
   - **Field Spells**: Affect both players and change the entire battlefield, often giving buffs or unique effects based on the theme of the deck.
   - **Quick-Play Spells**: Can be activated at any time, including during the opponent's turn, offering versatility and surprise.

3. **Trap Cards**: Trap cards are activated in response to an opponent's actions, allowing players to set up defenses or counterattacks. Traps can only be activated after being set face-down on the field and require careful timing.

   - **Normal Traps**: Similar to normal spells, these are one-time-use cards that go to the graveyard after activation.
   - **Continuous Traps**: These remain on the field and continuously impact the duel as long as they are active.
   - **Counter Traps**: The fastest type of trap, used to negate other card effects or summon attempts.

Mechanics of the Game

At its core, *Yu-Gi-Oh!* revolves around summoning monsters and using spells and traps to gain an advantage over your opponent. Here is a breakdown of the game flow:

1. **Start of the Duel**: Each player shuffles their deck and draws five cards. A coin flip or die roll determines who goes first.
2. **Phases of a Turn**:
    - **Draw Phase**: The player draws one card from their deck.
    - **Standby Phase**: Some card effects activate during this phase.
    - **Main Phase 1**: The player can summon monsters, activate spells, or set traps.
    - **Battle Phase**: The player can attack with monsters (if applicable).
    - **Main Phase 2**: Similar to Main Phase 1, players can summon or activate additional cards after the Battle Phase.
    - **End Phase**: The player's turn ends, and any effects that occur at the end of the turn resolve.
3. **Winning the Duel**: A player wins by reducing their opponent's Life Points to zero, making the opponent unable to draw from their deck, or meeting specific victory conditions set by certain cards.

Choosing the Right Gift Based on Game Knowledge

For those new to *Yu-Gi-Oh!*, a basic understanding of card types and mechanics will help you choose a gift that best suits the recipient. If the recipient is just starting out, a *Starter Deck* or *Structure Deck* is ideal. These pre-constructed decks provide everything a beginner needs to start dueling. If they're more advanced, *Booster Packs* and *Special Editions* offer a variety of new cards, giving them the excitement of opening packs and discovering rare or powerful additions to their collection.

This knowledge of card types and gameplay mechanics will allow you to tailor your gift selections to the recipient's level of expertise, ensuring you pick something meaningful, useful, and enjoyable for any *Yu-Gi-Oh!* fan.

Chapter 2: Starter Decks for Beginners

For newcomers to the *Yu-Gi-Oh!* trading card game, starter decks are the perfect way to ease into the game without being overwhelmed by the complexity of deck building or the variety of cards available. Starter decks are pre-constructed sets designed to introduce players to the basic mechanics of the game while offering a fun and engaging experience. In this chapter, we will explore what makes starter decks an excellent choice for beginners, highlight some of the most popular recent releases, and offer recommendations based on different playstyles.

What Are Starter Decks?

Starter decks are specifically curated to teach new players the core gameplay mechanics of *Yu-Gi-Oh!*. They typically contain a balanced mix of Monster, Spell, and Trap cards, with straightforward strategies that are easy to understand and execute. Unlike custom decks or competitive pre-built decks, starter decks prioritize simplicity, allowing players to focus on learning the game's fundamentals—such as summoning monsters, activating spells, setting traps, and managing resources—before moving on to more advanced strategies and combos.

These decks are designed to be ready to play right out of the box, making them the perfect gift for someone who is just starting their *Yu-Gi-Oh!* journey. In addition to being user-friendly, starter decks often feature some of the most iconic cards from the anime series, making them a great entry point for fans of the *Yu-Gi-Oh!* TV show or manga who want to get involved with the card game.

Why Starter Decks Are Ideal for Beginners

Starter decks are carefully designed with beginner-friendly cards that minimize confusion while teaching key concepts such as:

- **Basic Summoning**: New players will learn how to summon monsters in both attack and defense positions. Starter decks typically include Normal Monsters (without special effects) and Effect Monsters with simple abilities, allowing players to grasp the difference between the two types.
- **Spells and Traps**: Starter decks introduce essential Spell and Trap cards to teach the basic concepts of casting spells during your turn or setting traps to surprise your opponent.
- **Turn Structure**: Playing with a starter deck helps new duelists get accustomed to the different phases of a turn (Draw Phase, Main Phase, Battle Phase, etc.) and how to make decisions at each stage.
- **Deck Building Basics**: Although starter decks are pre-built, they give beginners insight into how decks are structured, such as maintaining a balance between Monster, Spell, and Trap cards. This knowledge will later help them when they start creating custom decks.

The structured nature of starter decks ensures that beginners can dive into the game without getting bogged down by complex rules or card interactions that might be too advanced at the early stages.

Popular Recent Starter Decks for Beginners

In recent years, Konami, the publisher of *Yu-Gi-Oh!*, has released several beginner-focused decks that offer an excellent mix of accessibility, fun, and a taste of the game's more advanced mechanics. Below are some highly recommended starter decks based on recent releases:

1. Starter Deck: Link Strike (2017)

The *Link Strike* Starter Deck was a landmark release, introducing players to one of the biggest changes in *Yu-Gi-Oh!* gameplay in years: Link Summoning. Link Monsters opened up a new dimension of strategy, and this deck is perfect for teaching new players how to use them effectively. The deck includes 45 cards, including staple cards for beginners such as *Cynet Universe* (a Field Spell that boosts Link Monsters) and *Link Spider* (a basic Link Monster that aids in quick summoning).

- **Key Features**:
    - Introduction to Link Summoning, a core mechanic in modern *Yu-Gi-Oh!*.
    - Includes a blend of Normal and Effect Monsters to help new players understand card effects.
    - A good balance between monsters and spells, allowing beginners to explore different card interactions.
- **Why it's Great for Beginners**: This deck simplifies the relatively new concept of Link Summoning, offering a smooth introduction to a mechanic that can become more complex in competitive play. It's also balanced in a way that teaches players how to combine Link Monsters with other types of monsters, enhancing their understanding of the Extra Deck.

2. Speed Duel Starter Decks: Duelists of Tomorrow (2019)

Speed Duel decks were designed for a quicker, more streamlined version of *Yu-Gi-Oh!*, making them perfect for beginners. The *Duelists of Tomorrow* set features characters from the original *Yu-Gi-Oh!* series, such as Yugi, Kaiba, and Joey, with themed decks for each. With only 20 cards per deck and simplified rules, Speed Duel decks offer a fast-paced introduction to the game without overwhelming new players with too many cards or complex effects.

- **Key Features**:
  - Themed decks based on iconic characters from the anime, which can appeal to fans of the show.
  - Simplified gameplay mechanics with fewer cards, allowing players to learn the basics quickly.
  - Each deck contains a mix of Normal and Effect Monsters, basic spells, and traps.
- **Why it's Great for Beginners**: The *Speed Duel* format is a scaled-down version of the full game, making it less intimidating for new players. It's an excellent choice for younger players or anyone who wants to learn the game at a faster pace. Plus, the familiar characters and cards from the anime give it a nostalgic feel.

3. Starter Deck: Codebreaker (2020)

Building on the *Link Strike* deck, the *Codebreaker* Starter Deck expands on Link Monsters and introduces players to more intricate strategies while still maintaining an easy learning curve. This 45-card deck includes powerful cards like *Decode Talker*, which has become a staple in Link Summoning strategies, as well as *RAM Clouder* and *Traffic Ghost*, helping players build a formidable Link strategy early on.

- **Key Features**:
    - A focus on Link Monsters with a solid mix of spells and traps to support summoning strategies.
    - Includes popular cards like *Linkuriboh*, which is easy to summon and serves as a great introduction to Link strategies.
    - Introduces some more advanced mechanics without being overly complicated for beginners.
- **Why it's Great for Beginners**: The *Codebreaker* deck is an excellent follow-up to the *Link Strike* Starter Deck, offering more depth while still being approachable for new players. It's ideal for beginners who have already learned the basics and want to start exploring more advanced mechanics.

4. Starter Deck: Yu-Gi-Oh! Speed Duel GX: Duel Academy Box (2022)

This Speed Duel set introduces players to the *Yu-Gi-Oh! GX* era, featuring decks themed around popular characters like Jaden Yuki and Zane Truesdale. Like other Speed Duel products, this set simplifies the game, with a reduced deck size and a quicker format, but introduces players to more advanced fusion mechanics and skill cards that replicate the abilities of GX characters.

- **Key Features**:
    - GX-themed decks that emphasize different playstyles and strategies.
    - Speed Duel format makes it easy to pick up and play without the complexities of a full game.
    - Includes skill cards that introduce a new layer of strategy by replicating the abilities of iconic GX characters.
- **Why it's Great for Beginners**: The Speed Duel format is perfect for newcomers, and this box set introduces them to the *Yu-Gi-Oh! GX* series, a fan-favorite era. The focus on themed characters and fusion mechanics provides variety, allowing beginners to experience different deck styles.

5. Structure Deck: Shaddoll Showdown (2020)

Although technically a structure deck, *Shaddoll Showdown* is a great option for beginners ready to dive a little deeper into the game's strategy while still maintaining a reasonable level of complexity. Shaddolls are an archetype of monsters that focus on flip effects (abilities that activate when the monster is flipped face-up from a face-down position), allowing players to learn the importance of timing and tactics. This deck includes powerful fusion monsters, giving beginners a glimpse into fusion summoning.

- **Key Features**:
    - Focus on flip effects, teaching players advanced timing and strategy.
    - Includes fusion monsters, offering an introduction to fusion summoning.
    - A pre-built deck that's easy to pick up but offers room for strategic growth.
- **Why it's Great for Beginners**: While slightly more advanced than a traditional starter deck, *Shaddoll Showdown* introduces more complex concepts like flip effects and fusion summoning in an accessible way. It's ideal for beginners who are ready to graduate from basic gameplay to more nuanced strategies.

Recommendations Based on Playstyle

- **For beginners who enjoy fast-paced games**: The *Speed Duel* starter decks (e.g., *Duelists of Tomorrow* and *GX: Duel Academy Box*) are perfect. These decks feature simplified rules and a faster gameplay format, making them ideal for quick learners or younger players.
- **For beginners interested in mastering new summoning techniques**: The *Link Strike* and *Codebreaker* starter decks are

excellent options, as they introduce the modern mechanic of Link Summoning, which is a key part of the current metagame.

- **For beginners who want a themed experience based on the anime**: The *Speed Duel* series, especially those based on characters from the original series or GX, offers a fun, nostalgic experience for fans of the *Yu-Gi-Oh!* TV show.
- **For those who want a more strategic challenge**: *Shaddoll Showdown* provides a more complex deck with fusion and flip mechanics, perfect for new players ready to delve deeper into strategy.

Conclusion

Starter decks provide the perfect entry point for new *Yu-Gi-Oh!* players, offering a balanced, accessible, and enjoyable introduction to the game. Whether you're selecting a deck based on iconic characters, new summoning mechanics, or streamlined formats, these decks ensure that new players can jump right into the world of dueling with confidence. With so many recent options available, you can easily find the ideal starter deck that suits the recipient's interests, giving them the tools to master the game and enjoy every duel along the way.

Chapter 3: Structure Decks for Advanced Players

As players progress from beginners to more experienced duelists, their desire for deeper strategies and more complex gameplay grows. While starter decks serve as an introduction to the *Yu-Gi-Oh!* Trading Card Game, structure decks are designed to take the experience to the next level. These pre-built themed decks are curated with more advanced strategies and combinations, catering to intermediate and advanced players who want to explore specific archetypes or mechanics. Structure decks offer a bridge between casual play and competitive deck building, making them an excellent choice for players looking to refine their skills or explore new strategies without starting from scratch.

In this chapter, we will explore the role of structure decks, examine why they are ideal for intermediate and advanced players, and highlight some of the most popular structure decks from recent releases. We'll also provide insights into why these decks make excellent gifts for seasoned *Yu-Gi-Oh!* players.

What Are Structure Decks?

Structure decks are pre-constructed decks that revolve around a specific theme, strategy, or archetype. Unlike starter decks, which focus on teaching basic game mechanics, structure decks are designed for players who already have a foundational understanding of the game and are looking for a more competitive edge. These decks often feature powerful combinations, intricate strategies, and synergies between cards, giving players the tools they need to compete at a higher level.

Structure decks typically come with around 40 to 50 cards, including monsters, spells, and traps that work harmoniously with the deck's central theme. They also often include Extra Deck monsters, such as

Fusion, Synchro, Xyz, or Link Monsters, to enhance the deck's versatility and power. Many structure decks are based on popular archetypes—groups of cards with shared themes and effects—which makes them highly collectible and enjoyable for players who want to build around specific strategies.

Why Structure Decks Are Perfect for Advanced Players

Structure decks provide a solid foundation for intermediate and advanced players to build upon. They offer a more complex and focused gameplay experience compared to starter decks, which are often too basic for experienced duelists. Here's why structure decks are ideal for players with more experience:

- **Advanced Synergies**: Structure decks are designed with intricate card synergies, encouraging players to explore more advanced tactics. These decks often rely on chaining effects, resource management, and specific summoning techniques that require a deeper understanding of the game.
- **Archetype Focus**: Each structure deck revolves around a central archetype, giving players the opportunity to master a specific set of cards and mechanics. This allows for a more cohesive deck-building experience, where each card is carefully selected to complement the theme.
- **Competitive Potential**: Many structure decks are strong enough to be used in competitive play, either as standalone decks or as a base for customization. With minor modifications, these decks can be optimized for local tournaments or even higher-level competitions.
- **Ready-to-Play**: Like starter decks, structure decks come ready-to-play out of the box. However, they provide much more depth and strategic potential, making them ideal for players who want to jump into more advanced gameplay without needing to build a deck from scratch.

- **Introduction to New Mechanics**: Structure decks often introduce players to advanced game mechanics, such as Fusion Summoning, Synchro Summoning, Xyz Summoning, and Link Summoning. These mechanics add layers of complexity and depth to the game, helping players expand their knowledge and improve their competitive skills.

Popular Structure Decks of Recent Years

In recent years, Konami has released several structure decks that have become highly popular among intermediate and advanced players. These decks offer a variety of playstyles, from aggressive monster-focused strategies to control decks that focus on limiting the opponent's moves. Below, we'll discuss some of the most successful structure decks from recent releases and what makes them stand out.

1. Structure Deck: Shaddoll Showdown (2020)

The *Shaddoll* archetype has been a fan favorite since its introduction, and the *Shaddoll Showdown* structure deck revitalized this classic archetype with updated cards and powerful combos. The deck focuses on *Shaddoll* monsters, which rely on Flip Effects (abilities that activate when the monster is flipped face-up) and Fusion Summoning. This deck allows players to chain effects together, quickly summoning powerful Fusion Monsters that can overwhelm opponents.

- **Key Features**:
    - Focus on *Shaddoll* Flip Effects, which teach players the importance of timing and tactical decision-making.
    - Introduces *El Shaddoll Construct* and *El Shaddoll Winda*, powerful Fusion Monsters that can dominate the battlefield.
    - Includes a range of versatile spell and trap cards that support the *Shaddoll* strategy.
- **Why It's Popular**: *Shaddoll Showdown* is beloved for its ability to balance offense and defense while relying on tactical gameplay.

The *Shaddoll* archetype's versatility allows players to create powerful combos while adapting to different situations, making this deck appealing for advanced players who want to master resource management and card effects.

2. Structure Deck: Sacred Beasts (2020)

For fans of the original *Yu-Gi-Oh!* series, the *Sacred Beasts* deck is a nostalgic powerhouse. This structure deck brings back the legendary Sacred Beasts—*Raviel, Lord of Phantasms, Hamon, Lord of Striking Thunder*, and *Uria, Lord of Searing Flames*—three incredibly powerful monsters with devastating abilities. The deck revolves around summoning these Sacred Beasts as quickly as possible while protecting them with spells and traps that enhance their power.

- **Key Features**:
    - Focuses on summoning high-attack monsters with formidable effects, making it an ideal choice for players who enjoy powerful, aggressive strategies.
    - Includes support cards like *Opening of the Spirit Gates* and *Awakening of the Sacred Beasts* to facilitate summoning the Sacred Beasts.
    - Can be customized to integrate other high-level monsters or improve consistency in summoning.
- **Why It's Popular**: The *Sacred Beasts* structure deck appeals to fans of the original series and players who enjoy summoning high-level monsters with game-changing effects. This deck is great for intermediate players who want to explore big-monster strategies and overwhelm their opponents with sheer power.

3. Structure Deck: Cyber Strike (2021)

The *Cyber Dragon* archetype has long been a staple in the *Yu-Gi-Oh!* competitive scene, and the *Cyber Strike* structure deck capitalizes on this legacy by combining *Cyber Dragon* strategies with *Cyberdark* monsters. This deck allows players to fuse their *Cyber* monsters into powerful Fusion Monsters like *Cyber End Dragon* and *Cyberdark Dragon*, while also supporting aggressive OTK (One-Turn Kill) strategies. It's perfect for players who enjoy explosive plays and fast-paced duels.

- **Key Features**:
    - Focuses on Fusion Summoning, utilizing cards like *Power Bond* and *Cybernetic Horizon* to bring out game-ending Fusion Monsters.
    - Offers multiple strategies, including aggressive OTK potential and control options with *Cyberdark* monsters.
    - Easily customizable, allowing players to enhance the deck with additional *Cyber* monsters or tech cards.
- **Why It's Popular**: *Cyber Strike* appeals to advanced players due to its versatility and competitive viability. The *Cyber Dragon* archetype is well-known for its ability to quickly summon massive monsters that can end games in a single turn. This deck offers a mix of nostalgia and modern gameplay, making it a favorite among advanced duelists.

4. Structure Deck: Ice Barrier of the Frozen Prison (2021)

The *Ice Barrier* archetype is known for its control-based strategies, focusing on locking down the opponent's moves and preventing them from executing their game plan. The *Ice Barrier of the Frozen Prison* structure deck revives this archetype with updated support and new Synchro Monsters that allow for a range of strategic plays. This deck is perfect for players who enjoy controlling the tempo of the game and outsmarting their opponents through calculated moves.

- **Key Features**:
    - Focus on control-based strategies, using *Ice Barrier* monsters to limit the opponent's ability to summon or attack.
    - Introduces powerful Synchro Monsters like *Trishula, Dragon of the Ice Barrier*, which can banish cards from the opponent's hand, field, and graveyard.
    - Includes support cards like *Freezing Chains of the Ice Barrier* and *Winds Over the Ice Barrier* to help with summoning.
- **Why It's Popular**: *Ice Barrier of the Frozen Prison* appeals to players who prefer a slower, more methodical playstyle. The deck's ability to control the field and disrupt the opponent's strategy makes it a favorite for duelists who enjoy outmaneuvering their opponents rather than relying on brute force.

5. Structure Deck: Albaz Strike (2022)

The *Albaz Strike* structure deck is centered around *Fallen of Albaz*, a monster that can fuse with the opponent's monsters to create powerful Fusion Monsters. This deck introduces the *Branded* archetype, which focuses on Fusion Summoning and controlling the battlefield by using the opponent's resources. The *Albaz Strike* deck is highly flexible and has seen success in competitive play, making it an excellent choice for advanced players looking to experiment with new strategies.

- **Key Features**:
  - Focus on Fusion Summoning, with *Fallen of Albaz* acting as the central card for Fusion plays.
  - Includes powerful Fusion Monsters like *Mirrorjade the Iceblade Dragon* and *Brigrand the Glory Dragon*, which can dominate the field.
  - Offers strong synergy with other archetypes, making it easy to customize and integrate into other decks.
- **Why It's Popular**: *Albaz Strike* is one of the most competitive structure decks released in recent years, offering a powerful and flexible strategy that can be customized for tournament play. The *Branded* archetype has become a fan favorite for its ability to control the field and create powerful Fusion Monsters by using the opponent's cards. This deck is ideal for advanced players who want to stay competitive while exploring new strategies.

Recommendations for Different Playstyles

- **For aggressive players**: The *Cyber Strike* and *Sacred Beasts* structure decks offer aggressive, high-powered strategies that focus on summoning massive monsters and overwhelming the opponent quickly.
- **For control-based players**: The *Ice Barrier of the Frozen Prison* structure deck is perfect for players who enjoy controlling the game's tempo and disrupting their opponent's strategy with calculated moves.
- **For fusion-focused players**: *Albaz Strike* and *Shaddoll Showdown* are ideal for players who love Fusion Summoning and creating powerful monsters that dominate the field.
- **For nostalgic fans**: The *Sacred Beasts* and *Cyber Strike* decks appeal to fans of the original series, offering a blend of nostalgia and competitive play.

Why Structure Decks Make Excellent Gifts

Structure decks are a fantastic gift for intermediate and advanced *Yu-Gi-Oh!* players because they offer a well-balanced and ready-to-play experience while providing the depth needed to enhance their gameplay. Whether the recipient is a casual player looking to explore new archetypes or a competitive duelist aiming to strengthen their strategy, structure decks provide the perfect balance between accessibility and advanced tactics.

Moreover, structure decks are highly collectible, often featuring cards from popular archetypes or themes that resonate with long-time fans. They are also easy to customize, giving players the flexibility to enhance the deck with additional cards to suit their playstyle. For anyone looking to give a thoughtful, engaging, and practical gift to a *Yu-Gi-Oh!*

fan, structure decks are a reliable choice that can bring excitement and new possibilities to their dueling experience.

In the next chapter, we'll dive deeper into the world of booster packs and tins, offering insights on how to expand a player's card collection and build on the foundation of starter and structure decks.

Chapter 4: Booster Packs for Collectors

For *Yu-Gi-Oh!* fans and collectors, few experiences can rival the excitement of opening a booster pack. The unpredictability, the possibility of pulling rare and valuable cards, and the thrill of expanding a collection make booster packs the perfect gift for anyone passionate about the *Yu-Gi-Oh!* Trading Card Game. Whether you're buying for a casual player who enjoys the surprise of new cards or a seasoned collector hunting for specific rares, booster packs offer endless possibilities for discovery. In this chapter, we will delve into the appeal of booster packs, explore some of the latest and most sought-after releases, and also discuss collectible tins that combine the excitement of booster packs with exclusive cards and practical storage.

What Are Booster Packs?

Booster packs are small, sealed packages of random *Yu-Gi-Oh!* cards that typically contain between 5 and 9 cards, depending on the set. Each pack includes a mix of commons, rares, super rares, ultra rares, and occasionally secret rares. What makes booster packs so enticing is their randomness—players never know exactly what they're going to get. This element of surprise, combined with the possibility of pulling highly sought-after cards, keeps fans coming back for more.

Booster packs are released in sets, with each set featuring a different theme, archetypes, and sometimes entirely new game mechanics. These releases often coincide with updates to the competitive metagame, providing new cards that help players build and enhance their decks. For collectors, booster packs offer a chance to find rare and valuable cards, including those with special holographic or alternate artwork, which can become the centerpiece of a collection.

Why Booster Packs Are Perfect for Collectors

Booster packs are ideal for collectors for several key reasons:

1. **Element of Surprise**: The random assortment of cards in each booster pack ensures that every opening is a unique experience. Collectors love the excitement of not knowing what they'll pull and the chance of finding something rare or valuable.

2. **Chase for Rarity**: Booster packs offer the opportunity to pull rare, ultra rare, secret rare, or even ghost rare cards. These cards are often more difficult to find, making them highly coveted by collectors who enjoy the challenge of completing their collection or acquiring valuable cards.

3. **Set Completion**: Many collectors aim to complete entire sets from specific booster releases. Opening multiple booster packs from a single set increases the likelihood of finding those last few missing cards needed to finish a collection.

4. **Investment Potential**: Certain rare cards, especially those pulled from older or limited booster packs, can increase in value over time. Collectors who invest in sealed booster packs or rare cards may find that their collection appreciates, making booster packs a great gift for collectors with an eye on long-term value.

5. **Customization and Expansion**: For players who also build and customize decks, booster packs provide fresh cards that can enhance their gameplay. Collectors who dabble in competitive play can use booster packs to find new cards that align with their strategies or archetypes.

Popular Recent Booster Packs for Collectors

In recent years, Konami has released several booster sets that have captured the attention of collectors. These sets feature a mix of new archetypes, reprints of classic cards, and the introduction of rare chase cards, making them particularly exciting for fans and collectors alike. Below are some of the most sought-after booster packs currently available, along with insights into what makes them special.

1. Duelist Nexus (2023)

Duelist Nexus is one of the standout booster sets from 2023, introducing new archetypes and providing significant support for existing ones like *Red-Eyes* and *Neos*. The set is particularly exciting for collectors due to the introduction of the *Transcend* monsters, a new type of Extra Deck monster that offers exciting new strategies and unique card designs. In addition to the new cards, *Duelist Nexus* includes highly coveted chase cards such as *Red-Eyes Soul Dragon* and *Transcendent Magician*, making it an appealing choice for collectors who are looking to pull rare and powerful cards.

- **Key Features**:
  - Introduction of the *Transcend* monster mechanic.
  - Support for popular archetypes like *Red-Eyes* and *Neos*.
  - Collectible secret rare and ultra rare cards that are highly sought after.
- **Why Collectors Love It**: The combination of new game mechanics and support for fan-favorite archetypes, along with the inclusion of rare chase cards, makes *Duelist Nexus* a must-have for collectors. The set's blend of nostalgia and innovation provides excitement for both seasoned players and collectors.

2. Photon Hypernova (2023)

Photon Hypernova is another major release from 2023 that offers significant support for the *Photon* and *Galaxy* archetypes, which first gained popularity during the *Yu-Gi-Oh! Zexal* era. The set contains some of the most visually stunning and highly collectible cards of the year, including secret rares like *Galaxy-Eyes Photon Lord* and *Starliege Photon Blast Dragon*. The focus on *Photon* and *Galaxy* monsters makes this set particularly appealing to fans of these archetypes, but the broader range of cards also provides value for any collector looking to expand their collection with beautiful and powerful cards.

- **Key Features**:
    - Focus on *Photon* and *Galaxy* archetypes with updated support.
    - Includes highly collectible secret rare and ultra rare cards.
    - Introduces new game-changing cards for competitive play.
- **Why Collectors Love It**: The stunning artwork and high rarity of certain cards, combined with the support for iconic archetypes, make *Photon Hypernova* a favorite among collectors. The set offers an exciting chance to pull rare and valuable cards, which are highly sought after in both casual and competitive circles.

3. Maze of Memories (2023)

For collectors who enjoy nostalgia, *Maze of Memories* is a dream come true. Released in 2023, this set focuses heavily on reprints of iconic cards from the original *Yu-Gi-Oh!* series, including fan favorites like *Gate Guardian* and *Kazejin*. In addition to reprints, *Maze of Memories* introduces new support cards for these classic monsters, giving collectors both new and old versions to chase. The set also includes highly collectible alternate artwork and secret rare versions of iconic cards, making it a valuable addition to any collector's stash.

- **Key Features**:
    - Reprints of classic cards from the original *Yu-Gi-Oh!* series.
    - New support cards for beloved monsters like *Gate Guardian*.
    - Highly collectible alternate artwork and secret rare cards.
- **Why Collectors Love It**: *Maze of Memories* taps into the nostalgia of longtime *Yu-Gi-Oh!* fans while offering new content and chase cards for collectors. The chance to pull rare reprints or secret rares from a set that pays homage to the early days of the game makes this a highly desirable pack for any collector.

4. Battle of Legend: Monstrous Revenge (2023)

The *Battle of Legend* series is known for introducing powerful reprints and highly collectible cards, and *Monstrous Revenge* is no exception. Released in 2023, this set includes a range of secret rare and ultra rare cards from older sets that have become hard to find. For collectors, *Monstrous Revenge* offers the opportunity to obtain rare reprints of valuable cards, such as *Exodia, the Forbidden One*, along with stunning new versions of other powerful monsters. The set also introduces new support for popular archetypes like *Sky Striker* and *Evil⬦Twin*, making it a well-rounded choice for both collectors and competitive players.

- **Key Features**:
  - Reprints of hard-to-find cards from previous sets.
  - Highly collectible secret rare and ultra rare cards, including fan favorites.
  - Support for competitive archetypes like *Sky Striker*.
- **Why Collectors Love It**: *Monstrous Revenge* offers a perfect mix of nostalgia, rarity, and competitive relevance, making it a top choice for collectors. The opportunity to pull rare and valuable cards from previous sets, along with the inclusion of stunning secret rare cards, ensures that this set remains in high demand.

5. Legendary Duelists: Soulburning Volcano (2023)

For fans of Fire-attribute monsters and the *Salamangreat* archetype, *Legendary Duelists: Soulburning Volcano* is an exciting booster set. Released in 2023, this set focuses heavily on Fire-attribute strategies and introduces new cards that enhance the *Salamangreat* archetype, a popular competitive deck. In addition to its competitive relevance, the set includes several highly collectible ultra rare and secret rare cards, making it appealing to both collectors and competitive players.

- **Key Features**:
    - Focus on Fire-attribute monsters and *Salamangreat* support.
    - Contains highly collectible ultra rare and secret rare cards.
    - Introduces new Fire-based strategies for competitive play.
- **Why Collectors Love It**: *Legendary Duelists: Soulburning Volcano* appeals to collectors who enjoy Fire-based archetypes or are fans of the *Salamangreat* cards. The set's rare and ultra rare cards, along with its competitive relevance, make it a valuable addition to any collection.

The Appeal of Yu-Gi-Oh! Tins

In addition to booster packs, collectible tins are another popular product for *Yu-Gi-Oh!* fans, offering both the excitement of booster packs and the practicality of card storage. *Yu-Gi-Oh!* tins are typically released annually and often feature some of the most sought-after cards from the year, packaged alongside multiple booster packs and exclusive promo cards. These tins are not only a great way to acquire valuable cards but also serve as a durable and stylish way to store and protect cards.

Why Tins Are Perfect for Collectors

1. **Exclusive Promo Cards**: Many *Yu-Gi-Oh!* tins come with exclusive promo cards that cannot be found in regular booster packs. These cards are often powerful or feature unique artwork, making them highly desirable for collectors.
2. **Multiple Booster Packs**: Each tin usually contains several booster packs from recent releases, giving collectors the chance to pull rare and valuable cards while enjoying the excitement of opening packs.
3. **High-Quality Storage**: The tins themselves are collectible and provide a practical way to store and protect cards. Many tins feature artwork of iconic monsters or themes from the *Yu-Gi-Oh!* universe, making them both functional and visually appealing.
4. **Investment Value**: Sealed tins often increase in value over time, especially if they contain exclusive cards or booster packs from limited-run sets. For collectors who enjoy investing in *Yu-Gi-Oh!*, keeping tins sealed can result in significant value appreciation.

Sought-After Yu-Gi-Oh! Tins

- **2022 Tin of the Pharaoh's Gods**: One of the most popular tins in recent years, this release featured iconic cards like *Blue-Eyes White Dragon* and *Dark Magician Girl*, as well as new support for several fan-favorite archetypes. The tin also included reprints of powerful meta-relevant cards, making it a top choice for collectors and players alike.
- **2023 Tin of Dueling Legends**: This tin became a hit with collectors due to its inclusion of exclusive promo cards featuring alternate artwork of beloved monsters like *Red-Eyes Black Dragon* and *Dark Magician*. It also contains booster packs from top sets of the year, including *Duelist Nexus* and *Photon Hypernova*, making it a valuable product for collectors.

Recommendations Based on Collecting Goals

- **For rare and iconic cards**: *Maze of Memories* and *Battle of Legend: Monstrous Revenge* offer a chance to pull reprints of classic cards, along with highly collectible secret rare versions.
- **For competitive and collectible value**: *Photon Hypernova* and *Duelist Nexus* are ideal for players who want to expand their decks with powerful cards while adding valuable collectibles to their collection.
- **For long-term collectors**: Tins like the *2022 Tin of the Pharaoh's Gods* and the *2023 Tin of Dueling Legends* offer exclusive promo cards and high-value booster packs, making them great gifts that can appreciate in value over time.

Why Booster Packs and Tins Make Excellent Gifts

Booster packs and tins are a perfect gift for any *Yu-Gi-Oh!* collector or player. Booster packs bring the excitement of discovery, with the potential to pull rare and valuable cards, while tins offer both exclusive content and practical storage solutions. Whether your recipient is a competitive player, a casual collector, or someone just beginning their *Yu-Gi-Oh!* journey, the thrill of opening a booster pack or a tin filled with surprises is sure to bring joy and excitement.

In the next chapter, we'll explore the world of *Yu-Gi-Oh!* memorabilia and merchandise, offering ideas for gifts that go beyond the trading card game and appeal to fans of the broader *Yu-Gi-Oh!* universe.

Chapter 5: Rare and Limited Edition Cards

For dedicated *Yu-Gi-Oh!* collectors and long-time fans, few items are as treasured as rare and limited-edition cards. These cards, often characterized by their scarcity, unique artwork, or historical significance, hold a special place in the *Yu-Gi-Oh!* Trading Card Game (TCG) community. Owning such cards not only adds value to a collection but also represents a connection to the rich history and evolution of the game. Whether they feature alternate art, are part of special promotional releases, or are ultra-rare chase cards, rare and limited-edition cards are highly coveted and often become the centerpiece of any serious collection.

This chapter will explore the world of rare and limited-edition *Yu-Gi-Oh!* cards, offering insights into how to find these prized possessions, how to identify authentic cards, and why they make exceptional gifts for fans and collectors. Whether you're a long-time fan seeking to expand your collection or a gift-giver looking for the perfect surprise for a *Yu-Gi-Oh!* enthusiast, understanding the appeal of rare cards will help you make an informed decision.

What Are Rare and Limited-Edition Cards?

Rare and limited-edition cards are special variants within the *Yu-Gi-Oh!* TCG that are more difficult to obtain than the standard cards found in most booster packs. These cards are typically released in limited quantities or as part of special promotions, making them much harder to find, thus increasing their value and desirability among collectors. Below are some of the main types of rare and limited-edition cards that collectors treasure:

- **Secret Rare**: Secret Rare cards are characterized by a rainbow-colored foil on the card's artwork and a shimmering foil on the card name. These cards are highly sought after due to their rarity and their stunning visual appearance.

- **Ultra Rare**: These cards feature gold foil names and holographic card art but lack the rainbow foil found in Secret Rares. Ultra Rare cards are commonly found in higher-level booster sets but are still highly valued, especially for iconic or powerful cards.
- **Ghost Rare**: One of the rarest card types, Ghost Rares are distinguished by their holographic, 3D-like artwork that makes the monster image appear ghostly. These cards are incredibly difficult to pull and are often released in very limited quantities.
- **Collector's Rare**: A newer rarity introduced in select sets, Collector's Rares feature a combination of gold foil and holographic backgrounds, giving the cards a unique visual texture. These are rare pulls, often reserved for highly anticipated sets.
- **Ultimate Rare**: Ultimate Rares have raised, embossed artwork, making them feel distinct from other cards. These are some of the rarest pulls in booster sets and are highly prized by collectors for both their rarity and texture.
- **Promo Cards**: Promo cards are released in conjunction with special events, tournaments, or products. These cards often feature alternate artwork or are printed in limited runs, making them difficult to find outside of the promotion period.
- **Tournament Prize Cards**: Some of the rarest *Yu-Gi-Oh!* cards are tournament prize cards, which are awarded only to the top players in high-level competitions such as World Championships or National Tournaments. These cards are often one-of-a-kind or part of extremely limited runs, making them some of the most valuable cards in existence.
- **Limited Edition**: Limited-edition cards are often included in special collector's tins, promotional products, or special sets. They are printed in smaller quantities than regular cards, making them a great find for collectors who value exclusivity.

Why Rare and Limited-Edition Cards Are Prized by Collectors

The allure of rare and limited-edition cards lies in several factors that appeal to collectors:

1. **Scarcity**: The harder a card is to find, the more desirable it becomes. Many rare cards are produced in limited quantities or only available during specific events or promotional periods. Their scarcity makes them highly collectible, with some cards becoming legendary in the community for their rarity alone.

2. **Visual Appeal**: Rare cards often feature special foiling, holographic effects, or alternate artwork that sets them apart from standard cards. Collector's Rares, Ghost Rares, and Ultimate Rares are particularly beautiful and offer a level of visual craftsmanship that enhances their desirability.

3. **Historical Significance**: Certain rare cards have become iconic over the years due to their role in major tournaments, their presence in the *Yu-Gi-Oh!* anime, or their historical importance in the TCG. For example, cards like *Dark Magician* and *Blue-Eyes White Dragon* in rare formats are deeply tied to the origins of the game and hold a special place in fans' hearts.

4. **Investment Value**: Rare *Yu-Gi-Oh!* cards can increase in value over time, especially if they are part of limited releases or promotional sets. Collectors often invest in rare cards with the hope that their value will appreciate, making them both a hobby and a potential financial investment.

5. **Exclusivity**: Owning a rare card, especially one that was part of a limited run or awarded only to top tournament players, grants a sense of exclusivity. These cards become personal trophies in a collection, representing a collector's dedication to the game.

How to Find Rare and Limited-Edition Cards

Finding rare and limited-edition *Yu-Gi-Oh!* cards requires patience, research, and sometimes a little luck. Here are some tips for locating these prized possessions:

1. **Special Releases and Tins**: Keep an eye on special *Yu-Gi-Oh!* product releases, such as collectible tins, anniversary sets, and limited-edition booster sets. These products often contain exclusive promo cards or limited-edition cards that are not available in standard booster packs. For example, tins like the *2022 Tin of the Pharaoh's Gods* or *2023 Tin of Dueling Legends* include highly sought-after cards and exclusive content that appeal to collectors.

2. **Booster Packs with High Rarity Pull Rates**: Some booster packs are known for their higher chances of pulling rare cards. Sets like *Battle of Legend: Monstrous Revenge* or *Duelist Nexus* often include ultra-rare or secret rare cards that are prized by collectors. Purchasing sealed booster boxes or cases increases the likelihood of obtaining rare cards.

3. **Online Marketplaces**: Websites such as eBay, TCGPlayer, and CardMarket are great platforms for finding rare and limited-edition *Yu-Gi-Oh!* cards. Many sellers offer graded and authenticated cards, ensuring that you are purchasing legitimate, high-quality items. However, prices for rare cards on these platforms can vary widely, so it's essential to research the market value before making a purchase.

4. **Card Shops and Conventions**: Local card shops and gaming conventions are excellent places to find rare cards. Many shops carry singles of rare cards, and conventions often feature vendors who specialize in high-end collectibles. Additionally, conventions like *Yu-Gi-Oh! Championship Series* (YCS) events sometimes fea-

ture exclusive promotional cards that can only be obtained by attending.

5. **Trading with Other Collectors**: One of the traditional ways to find rare cards is by trading with other collectors. Many serious collectors have extensive inventories of rare and limited-edition cards and may be willing to trade duplicates for cards they need. Platforms like TCGPlayer also feature trade forums where collectors can exchange cards.

How to Identify Authentic Rare Cards

As the market for rare and limited-edition *Yu-Gi-Oh!* cards grows, so does the risk of encountering counterfeit cards. To ensure that you are purchasing authentic cards, follow these tips:

1. **Inspect the Card's Printing**: Authentic *Yu-Gi-Oh!* cards have specific design elements, including the iconic *Yu-Gi-Oh!* card back, accurate colors, and high-quality foiling. Fake cards often have slightly off-color printing or blurred text. The foil effect on rare cards should be consistent and smooth, not overly shiny or uneven.

2. **Check the Card's Texture**: Genuine rare cards, especially Ultimate Rares and Ghost Rares, have distinct textures. Ultimate Rares have raised and embossed artwork, while Ghost Rares have a ghostly 3D effect. Counterfeit cards may lack these details or have inconsistent texturing.

3. **Examine the Hologram**: Each legitimate *Yu-Gi-Oh!* card contains a small hologram in the lower right-hand corner of the card. For cards printed after 2002, this hologram is a silver or gold square with the *Yu-Gi-Oh!* logo. If this hologram is missing or looks tampered with, the card may be a fake.

4. **Use Grading and Authentication Services**: Services like PSA (Professional Sports Authenticator) and Beckett offer grading and authentication services for rare cards. If you're unsure about

the authenticity of a card, submitting it to a grading service will provide you with a certified, graded card that has been verified as authentic. Graded cards are also sealed in tamper-proof cases, which help preserve their condition.

5. **Buy from Reputable Sellers**: When purchasing rare cards, always buy from reputable sources, such as established card shops, verified online sellers, or trusted collectors. Reputable sellers are more likely to provide guarantees or return policies, ensuring you receive legitimate cards.

Why Rare and Limited-Edition Cards Make Excellent Gifts

Rare and limited-edition *Yu-Gi-Oh!* cards make exceptional gifts for several reasons:

- **Sentimental Value**: For long-time fans and collectors, receiving a rare card, especially one tied to a favorite archetype or character, is deeply meaningful. Cards like alternate artwork versions of *Dark Magician* or *Blue-Eyes White Dragon* can evoke nostalgia and bring joy to collectors.

- **Investment Potential**: Rare cards often increase in value over time, making them a thoughtful gift that can appreciate in worth. For collectors who are also investors, receiving a valuable or limited-edition card can be both a sentimental and financial asset.

- **Display Worthiness**: Many rare cards are visually stunning and serve as excellent display pieces. For serious collectors, rare cards often become the centerpiece of a collection, and gifting a rare card offers the recipient something they can proudly show off.

- **Personalized Gift**: Knowing what cards are important to the recipient's collection allows for a more personalized gift. Whether it's a rare card from their favorite archetype or a promo card from a tournament they've always admired, rare cards can be a highly personal and thoughtful present.

Conclusion

Rare and limited-edition *Yu-Gi-Oh!* cards represent the pinnacle of collecting for many fans. Whether it's the allure of owning a scarce card, the beauty of holographic artwork, or the excitement of completing a collection, rare cards offer a sense of accomplishment and pride. By understanding how to find and identify these cards, as well as why they are so valued, you can make informed decisions when purchasing rare cards for yourself or as a gift for others. These prized cards not only hold sentimental and aesthetic value but also represent the rich history and ongoing legacy of the *Yu-Gi-Oh!* TCG.

In the next chapter, we will explore the world of *Yu-Gi-Oh!* memorabilia and other collectibles, offering insight into how to extend a fan's passion for the game beyond the cards themselves.

Chapter 6: Playmats and Accessories

While the heart of *Yu-Gi-Oh!* lies in the cards themselves, experienced duelists know that having the right accessories can elevate their gaming experience, adding both functionality and style to their gameplay. Playmats, card sleeves, and deck boxes are not just practical tools for protecting cards and organizing decks—they also offer players a chance to express their personal style, protect their valuable cards, and enhance the enjoyment of the game. For collectors and competitive players alike, these accessories make thoughtful and practical gifts that complement their love for the *Yu-Gi-Oh!* Trading Card Game (TCG).

In this chapter, we'll explore the world of *Yu-Gi-Oh!* accessories, including custom playmats, protective card sleeves, deck boxes, and other useful items that players value. Whether you're looking for a functional gift or something that allows a player to showcase their style, these accessories offer a perfect blend of practicality and personality.

The Importance of Accessories in Yu-Gi-Oh!

Accessories are an essential part of any *Yu-Gi-Oh!* player's toolkit. Not only do they serve to protect a player's valuable cards from wear and tear, but they also create a more enjoyable and organized playing experience. High-quality accessories can make a big difference in the longevity of a collection and the ease of gameplay. For serious players, these accessories are as important as the cards themselves.

Here are some of the main reasons why accessories are crucial:

- **Card Protection**: Cards, especially rare or holographic ones, can wear down over time due to constant handling. Card sleeves and deck boxes protect cards from dirt, scratches, and damage, preserving their value and playability.
- **Enhanced Gameplay**: Playmats provide a smooth surface for dueling, reducing the chances of cards sliding off the table or getting

damaged during play. Playmats also help players organize their field zones and keep their cards in neat order.

- **Personal Expression**: Many players take pride in customizing their setup with accessories that reflect their favorite cards, archetypes, or anime characters. Custom playmats, themed card sleeves, and deck boxes offer players a way to show off their personality and passion for the game.

- **Organization**: With a large collection of cards, players need to keep their decks and extra cards organized. Deck boxes allow for neat storage and easy transportation, ensuring that cards stay in top condition between games.

Playmats: Functionality and Style in One

A playmat is one of the most important accessories for a *Yu-Gi-Oh!* player, providing a dedicated space for cards during duels and protecting them from rough surfaces. Playmats are typically made of soft, durable materials like neoprene or fabric with a rubber backing to prevent slipping. They often feature artwork of iconic monsters or characters, adding a stylish element to gameplay.

Why Playmats Make a Great Gift

- **Card Protection**: A good playmat protects cards from dirt, rough surfaces, and moisture, helping to keep them in mint condition even during intense duels. This is particularly important for rare or expensive cards that players want to preserve.

- **Enhanced Organization**: Playmats often have pre-marked zones that correspond to different parts of the *Yu-Gi-Oh!* game (Monster Zone, Spell/Trap Zone, Extra Deck Zone, etc.). This helps players stay organized and ensures they place their cards correctly during a duel.

- **Personalization and Style**: Custom playmats offer players a chance to express their unique style or allegiance to a favorite archetype or character. Many playmats feature stunning artwork from the *Yu-Gi-Oh!* anime or showcase popular monsters like *Dark Magician*, *Blue-Eyes White Dragon*, or *Exodia the Forbidden One*. Some players even commission personalized playmats with custom artwork, creating a one-of-a-kind accessory.

- **Durability**: A high-quality playmat is built to last, withstanding years of use. This makes it a practical gift that players will use over and over again, whether at home or in competitive settings.

Popular Playmats for Yu-Gi-Oh! Players

1. **Official Yu-Gi-Oh! Playmats**: These playmats are often released during special events, tournaments, or promotions, featuring artwork of popular cards and characters from the series. They are a great choice for fans who want to represent their favorite card in style.

2. **Custom Playmats**: Many online retailers offer custom playmats where players can choose their own designs, colors, and artwork. Some vendors even allow customers to upload their own artwork for a truly personalized mat. Custom playmats are perfect for players who want to create something unique.

3. **Anime-Themed Playmats**: Playmats featuring artwork from the *Yu-Gi-Oh!* anime are a popular choice among fans. These mats often showcase famous duels or characters like Yugi, Kaiba, or Seto Kaiba's signature monsters, making them an attractive gift for fans of the show.

4. **Tournament-Exclusive Playmats**: Playmats given as prizes at *Yu-Gi-Oh!* Championship Series (YCS) events or other official tournaments are often rare and highly sought after. If you're looking for a high-end gift for a competitive player, a limited-edition tournament playmat can be a valuable addition to their collection.

Card Sleeves: Protection with Style

Card sleeves are essential for anyone serious about preserving their *Yu-Gi-Oh!* cards. Sleeves protect cards from scratches, dirt, and wear that occur during shuffling and handling. They are especially important for valuable or rare cards, which can lose value if they become damaged. Beyond protection, card sleeves offer players a way to customize their deck with designs that reflect their personal style or favorite cards.

Why Card Sleeves Make a Great Gift

- **Card Preservation**: Sleeves help prevent damage to cards, especially during shuffling and gameplay. For rare or high-value cards, this is critical in maintaining their condition and value.
- **Customization**: Card sleeves come in a wide variety of designs, from simple transparent sleeves to sleeves featuring intricate artwork of popular cards or anime characters. This allows players to express their individuality or showcase their allegiance to a particular archetype or theme.
- **Improved Shuffling**: Sleeves make shuffling smoother and less damaging to cards, which is important for competitive players who frequently shuffle their decks during matches.

Popular Types of Card Sleeves

1. **Official Yu-Gi-Oh! Sleeves**: Konami releases official *Yu-Gi-Oh!* card sleeves featuring popular monsters or artwork from the series. These sleeves are often sold in conjunction with new booster sets or special events, making them a great collectible gift.
2. **Custom Sleeves**: Many companies offer custom-designed card sleeves, allowing players to choose designs that match their favorite archetypes or characters. These sleeves often feature high-

quality artwork and are perfect for players who want a unique look for their decks.

3. **Tournament Sleeves**: Like playmats, some tournaments offer exclusive card sleeves as prizes or giveaways. These are often rare and can be highly sought after by collectors and competitive players alike.

4. **Character-Themed Sleeves**: Sleeves featuring artwork of characters like Yugi, Kaiba, or Joey are always popular among fans of the anime. They make for a fun and personal gift for players who are also fans of the *Yu-Gi-Oh!* TV series.

Deck Boxes: Organize and Protect Your Cards

Deck boxes are essential for players who want to keep their cards organized and protected when traveling to tournaments, events, or casual play sessions. A high-quality deck box ensures that cards are kept in pristine condition between duels, and many deck boxes are designed to hold sleeved cards, making them perfect for players who take their card protection seriously.

Why Deck Boxes Make a Great Gift

- **Card Protection**: A sturdy deck box prevents cards from being bent, scratched, or damaged while in transit. This is especially important for players who travel with their decks or frequently play at events.

- **Organization**: Deck boxes keep decks organized and separated, preventing cards from becoming mixed up or lost. For players with multiple decks, deck boxes are a must-have for keeping everything in order.

- **Stylish Designs**: Deck boxes come in a wide variety of designs, from sleek, minimalist cases to elaborately decorated boxes featuring *Yu-Gi-Oh!* artwork. This gives players the opportunity to choose a deck box that matches their personal style or favorite cards.

Popular Types of Deck Boxes

1. **Leather or Faux-Leather Deck Boxes**: These high-end deck boxes are perfect for serious players who want a durable and stylish way to protect their cards. Leather deck boxes often come with magnetic closures and are designed to hold multiple decks or extra accessories.

2. **Official Yu-Gi-Oh! Deck Boxes**: Konami produces official deck boxes featuring popular *Yu-Gi-Oh!* monsters, characters, and themes. These deck boxes are a great gift for fans who want to showcase their love for the game while keeping their cards safe.

3. **Custom and Themed Deck Boxes**: Many online retailers offer custom deck boxes with designs based on specific archetypes or personal artwork. These boxes are ideal for players who want a unique accessory that stands out from the crowd.

4. **Double or Multi-Deck Boxes**: For players who carry multiple decks to tournaments or events, double or multi-deck boxes are a practical gift. These boxes are designed to hold two or more decks, as well as extra cards or accessories like dice and tokens.

Other Accessories That Make Great Gifts

Beyond playmats, sleeves, and deck boxes, there are a variety of other accessories that can enhance a *Yu-Gi-Oh!* player's experience:

1. **Dice and Counters**: Many players use dice or counters to keep track of Life Points, counters on cards, or token monsters during a duel. Custom dice featuring *Yu-Gi-Oh!* symbols or characters make a fun and useful gift.

2. **Binder or Card Album**: For collectors, a high-quality binder or card album is essential for organizing and displaying their collection. Look for binders with high-capacity sleeves and sturdy construction to ensure cards are kept safe.

3. **Card Dividers**: Card dividers help players organize their decks and sideboards within deck boxes or binders. These dividers often feature artwork or designs that match specific archetypes or themes, making them a small but thoughtful gift.

Why Playmats and Accessories Make Excellent Gifts

Accessories like playmats, card sleeves, and deck boxes make excellent gifts for *Yu-Gi-Oh!* players for several reasons:

- **Practicality**: These items are essential for any serious player or collector, helping to protect cards, enhance gameplay, and keep everything organized.
- **Customization**: With so many designs and options available, it's easy to find accessories that match a player's personal style or favorite archetype. Custom playmats, sleeves, and deck boxes allow for personalization, making the gift even more special.
- **Durability**: High-quality accessories are built to last, meaning that the recipient can enjoy their gift for years to come. Whether it's a durable playmat or a sturdy deck box, these items will be used regularly and appreciated.
- **Versatility**: Playmats and accessories can be used in a variety of settings, from casual home play to competitive tournaments, making them a versatile gift for any player.

Conclusion

Playmats, card sleeves, and deck boxes are more than just accessories—they are essential tools that help *Yu-Gi-Oh!* players protect their cards, express their personal style, and enhance their overall gameplay experience. These functional and stylish items make thoughtful and practical gifts for both casual players and serious collectors. With a wide range of designs, themes, and custom options, it's easy to find the perfect accessory that will add excitement and personality to any player's *Yu-Gi-Oh!* setup.

In the next chapter, we'll explore *Yu-Gi-Oh!* memorabilia and merchandise, offering ideas for gifts that go beyond the cards and appeal to fans of the broader *Yu-Gi-Oh!* universe. Whether it's apparel, action figures, or collectible statues, there's a wealth of options for *Yu-Gi-Oh!* enthusiasts who want to display their love for the game in every aspect of their life.

Chapter 7: Yu-Gi-Oh! Memorabilia and Merchandise

While the *Yu-Gi-Oh!* Trading Card Game (TCG) is at the heart of the fandom, the franchise has expanded far beyond the cards, encompassing a wide variety of memorabilia and merchandise that appeal to fans of all ages. From apparel and action figures to collectible statues and home decor, *Yu-Gi-Oh!* enthusiasts can celebrate their love for the game in many ways beyond the dueling table. For long-time fans and collectors, *Yu-Gi-Oh!* merchandise offers a way to showcase their passion for the series and its iconic characters.

In this chapter, we'll explore a range of *Yu-Gi-Oh!* memorabilia and merchandise that make excellent gift ideas for fans who want to take their love for the franchise beyond the TCG. Whether you're shopping for a casual fan, a hardcore collector, or someone who grew up watching the anime, there's a wealth of *Yu-Gi-Oh!* products that bring the magic of dueling to everyday life.

The Appeal of Yu-Gi-Oh! Merchandise

Merchandise based on the *Yu-Gi-Oh!* universe goes beyond the cards, offering fans an opportunity to express their love for the franchise in more personal and creative ways. Whether it's wearing a t-shirt with their favorite monster, displaying an action figure of their beloved character, or collecting limited-edition statues, *Yu-Gi-Oh!* merchandise allows fans to incorporate the series into their daily lives.

Here's why *Yu-Gi-Oh!* memorabilia and merchandise are so appealing to fans:

1. **Nostalgia and Fandom**: Many *Yu-Gi-Oh!* fans grew up watching the anime or playing the TCG, and merchandise allows them to reconnect with their favorite characters, monsters, and memories from the series. Owning collectibles that feature *Yugi*, *Kaiba*, or iconic monsters like *Blue-Eyes White Dragon* brings back feelings of nostalgia and joy.

2. **Personal Expression**: *Yu-Gi-Oh!* fans take pride in their love for the franchise, and merchandise offers them a way to showcase

that fandom. Whether it's through apparel, posters, or collectible figurines, fans can display their enthusiasm for *Yu-Gi-Oh!* in unique and creative ways.

3. **Collectibility**: Just like the TCG, *Yu-Gi-Oh!* memorabilia often holds value and can become highly collectible over time. Limited-edition figures, statues, and exclusive promotional items are highly sought after by collectors, making them perfect gifts for those who enjoy building collections.

4. **Diverse Options**: The world of *Yu-Gi-Oh!* merchandise is vast and diverse, with options ranging from practical items like clothing and accessories to high-end collectibles such as action figures and statues. This variety ensures that there's something for everyone, whether they're a casual fan or a serious collector.

Apparel: Show Off Your Fandom in Style

One of the most popular ways fans express their love for *Yu-Gi-Oh!* is through apparel. Clothing items such as t-shirts, hoodies, hats, and accessories allow fans to wear their fandom with pride while incorporating it into their everyday style. Many *Yu-Gi-Oh!* apparel items feature iconic characters, monsters, or logos, making them fun and fashionable gifts for fans of the series.

Why Yu-Gi-Oh! Apparel Makes a Great Gift

- **Everyday Wear**: *Yu-Gi-Oh!* apparel allows fans to showcase their love for the series in a way that's easy and practical. A t-shirt featuring the *Millennium Puzzle* or a hoodie with *Kaiba's Blue-Eyes White Dragon* can be worn on casual outings or at gaming events.

- **Variety of Designs**: There's a wide range of *Yu-Gi-Oh!* designs available, from minimalist logos to bold, colorful graphics featuring popular characters and monsters. Whether someone prefers a subtle nod to the franchise or a full-on character portrait, there's a design for every fan.

• **Great for Fans of All Ages**: Apparel is a versatile gift that appeals to fans of all ages, whether they grew up with the original series or are newer fans of the game. T-shirts, hats, and hoodies make great gifts for both younger fans and adult collectors.

Popular Apparel Items for Yu-Gi-Oh! Fans

1. **Character T-Shirts**: T-shirts featuring fan-favorite characters like *Yugi*, *Kaiba*, and *Joey* are among the most popular *Yu-Gi-Oh!* apparel items. These shirts often include vibrant artwork of the characters along with iconic monsters like *Dark Magician* and *Red-Eyes Black Dragon*.

2. **Monster-Themed Hoodies**: Hoodies featuring iconic monsters such as *Blue-Eyes White Dragon*, *Dark Magician Girl*, or *Exodia the Forbidden One* are perfect for colder weather and make stylish gifts for any fan. These designs typically incorporate bold graphics that stand out in any setting.

3. **Millennium Item Accessories**: For fans of the ancient Egyptian themes in *Yu-Gi-Oh!*, accessories such as hats, beanies, or jewelry featuring the *Millennium Puzzle* or other Millennium Items are popular. These items offer a subtle nod to the franchise while still being fashionable.

Action Figures: Bring Yu-Gi-Oh! Characters to Life

For fans who want to bring their favorite *Yu-Gi-Oh!* characters to life, action figures are an exciting collectible option. Action figures are highly detailed, poseable models that represent characters and monsters from the anime and TCG. These figures often come with accessories like weapons, interchangeable hands, or cards, allowing fans to recreate famous scenes from the anime or set up dynamic displays.

Why Action Figures Make a Great Gift

- **High Collectibility**: Action figures are often part of limited-edition releases or specific lines, making them highly collectible. Fans who enjoy collecting memorabilia will appreciate the rarity and craftsmanship of these figures.
- **Display Value**: Action figures are designed to be displayed, whether on a collector's shelf or as part of a larger diorama. For fans who enjoy curating their own *Yu-Gi-Oh!* displays, action figures offer the perfect way to bring their favorite characters and monsters to life.
- **Nostalgic Appeal**: Many action figures are based on characters from the original anime, making them especially appealing to long-time fans who want to relive their favorite moments from the series.

Popular Yu-Gi-Oh! Action Figures

1. **Figma Yami Yugi Action Figure**: This highly detailed and poseable figure of *Yami Yugi*, the protagonist of the original series, is a favorite among collectors. It includes accessories like the *Millennium Puzzle* and *Duel Disk*, as well as multiple facial expressions, allowing fans to recreate iconic scenes from the anime.

2. **Kaiba Corp. Blue-Eyes White Dragon Figure**: Fans of *Seto Kaiba* and his iconic *Blue-Eyes White Dragon* will love the collectible figures of this legendary monster. These figures often feature detailed, dynamic poses that capture the majesty and power of the *Blue-Eyes*.

3. **Duelist Kingdom Joey Wheeler Action Figure**: For fans of Joey Wheeler, this action figure from the *Duelist Kingdom* arc

features Joey with his classic deck of cards and accessories. The figure includes interchangeable parts and offers poseable joints, making it a great addition to any *Yu-Gi-Oh!* collection.

Collectible Statues: High-End Display Pieces

For serious collectors, high-end collectible statues represent the pinnacle of *Yu-Gi-Oh!* memorabilia. These statues are typically larger and more detailed than action figures, often hand-painted and sculpted to perfection. They capture iconic characters and monsters in dynamic poses, making them perfect for display in a collection or as a centerpiece in a fan's home.

Why Collectible Statues Make a Great Gift

- **Premium Quality**: Collectible statues are often crafted with high-quality materials such as resin or PVC and are hand-painted for maximum detail. These statues are designed to be long-lasting, making them a luxurious and special gift.
- **Impressive Display Pieces**: Due to their larger size and intricate details, collectible statues make an impressive statement in any room. Fans who love to showcase their *Yu-Gi-Oh!* collection will appreciate the craftsmanship and presence of these statues.
- **Exclusive Releases**: Many collectible statues are part of limited-edition releases, making them rare and valuable. For a serious collector, owning a limited-edition statue adds significant prestige to their collection.

Popular Yu-Gi-Oh! Statues

1. **Kotobukiya Dark Magician 1/7 Scale Statue**: This highly detailed statue of *Dark Magician* captures the iconic monster in a dynamic, spell-casting pose. The intricate details and hand-painted finish make this statue a prized piece for collectors, and it stands out as a centerpiece in any display.

2. **First 4 Figures Blue-Eyes White Dragon Statue**: For fans of *Seto Kaiba* and *Blue-Eyes White Dragon*, this statue is an awe-inspiring depiction of the legendary monster. Featuring a majestic pose with its wings spread wide, the *Blue-Eyes* statue is a must-have for serious collectors.

3. **Yami Yugi Millennium Puzzle Figure**: This limited-edition statue of *Yami Yugi* holding the *Millennium Puzzle* is a stunning representation of the series' protagonist. It features incredible attention to detail, capturing the spirit and intensity of Yugi in full duelist mode.

Home Decor and Miscellaneous Merchandise

For fans looking to bring a touch of *Yu-Gi-Oh!* into their everyday life, there are plenty of home decor items and miscellaneous merchandise that make great gifts. These products range from practical items to unique collectibles, offering fans a chance to integrate *Yu-Gi-Oh!* into their daily routines.

Why Home Decor and Miscellaneous Merchandise Make Great Gifts

- **Functional and Fun**: Many *Yu-Gi-Oh!* home decor items serve a functional purpose while also showcasing the franchise's iconic imagery. From bedding to posters, these items are perfect for fans who want to bring the magic of *Yu-Gi-Oh!* into their everyday spaces.

- **Unique and Creative**: Home decor and miscellaneous merchandise often feature creative designs and artwork, making them fun and thoughtful gifts for fans. Items like lamps, mugs, and posters can be used or displayed in a fan's home or office, adding a touch of their favorite series to their surroundings.

Popular Yu-Gi-Oh! Home Decor and Merchandise

1. **Yu-Gi-Oh! Posters and Wall Art**: Posters featuring artwork from the anime or the TCG are a great way for fans to decorate their space. From classic duels to monster art, posters allow fans to bring their favorite scenes to life on their walls.
2. **Millennium Puzzle Lamp**: This creative and functional lamp is shaped like the *Millennium Puzzle* and adds a soft glow to any room. It's a unique piece of decor that appeals to fans of the series' ancient Egyptian themes.
3. **Yu-Gi-Oh! Themed Mugs**: Mugs featuring designs of iconic monsters or characters are a fun way for fans to enjoy their morning coffee while thinking about their next duel.
4. **Yu-Gi-Oh! Bedding and Blankets**: For young fans or die-hard collectors, bedding sets and blankets featuring designs of popular characters or monsters make a fun and cozy gift.

Why Yu-Gi-Oh! Memorabilia and Merchandise Make Excellent Gifts

Yu-Gi-Oh! memorabilia and merchandise offer a diverse range of gift options that go beyond the trading card game. From stylish apparel to collectible figures and unique home decor, these items allow fans to celebrate their love for the franchise in fun and creative ways. Whether you're looking for a rare collectible statue or a practical item like a themed mug, *Yu-Gi-Oh!* merchandise makes for thoughtful, personalized gifts that fans will treasure.

In the next chapter, we'll focus on combining the perfect *Yu-Gi-Oh!* gifts to create a thoughtful package for different types of fans, from casual players to serious collectors. Whether it's a mix of booster packs, accessories, or memorabilia, we'll guide you through the best ways to surprise and delight the *Yu-Gi-Oh!* fan in your life.

Chapter 8: Collector's Boxes and Tins

For *Yu-Gi-Oh!* fans and collectors, few gifts are as exciting and versatile as collector's boxes and tins. These special editions are designed to bring together the best of the *Yu-Gi-Oh!* experience by offering not only booster packs but also exclusive promotional cards, collectible tins, and other rare items that enhance both a player's collection and gameplay. Whether you're shopping for a casual player or a dedicated collector, these sets offer a comprehensive package filled with exciting surprises and high value, making them the perfect gift for any *Yu-Gi-Oh!* enthusiast.

In this chapter, we'll explore the appeal of collector's boxes and tins, examine what makes them such desirable gift options, and highlight some of the most popular releases from recent years. We'll also provide guidance on how to choose the best set based on the recipient's interests, whether they're a competitive player, a casual duelist, or a long-time collector.

What Are Collector's Boxes and Tins?

Collector's boxes and tins are special *Yu-Gi-Oh!* products that typically bundle together a variety of items, including booster packs, limited-edition promo cards, and collectible tins or boxes. These products are often released to celebrate major events in the *Yu-Gi-Oh!* universe—such as anniversaries, tournaments, or new expansions—and are designed to offer players a premium experience with exclusive content that can't be found in standard booster packs.

Collector's boxes and tins are highly sought after by both players and collectors for several reasons:

- **Exclusive Promo Cards**: Many collector's sets include limited-edition promo cards that are not available in regular booster packs. These cards often feature alternate artwork or special foil finishes, making them a valuable addition to any collection.

- **Booster Packs**: Each collector's tin or box typically comes with several booster packs from recent or classic sets, giving players the thrill of opening new cards and expanding their collection.

- **Storage and Display**: The tins and boxes themselves are often designed with collectible artwork and are durable enough to be used for storing decks, cards, or other gaming accessories. These tins make for attractive display pieces, adding an extra layer of value to the set.

- **Great Value**: For the price, collector's boxes and tins offer a great deal of value. They provide a variety of items in one package—cards, packs, and storage—making them an ideal gift for any *Yu-Gi-Oh!* fan.

Why Collector's Boxes and Tins Make Excellent Gifts

Collector's boxes and tins are more than just a bundle of cards and booster packs—they offer a comprehensive experience that appeals to both players and collectors. Here's why they make such excellent gifts:

1. **All-in-One Package**: Collector's tins and boxes are carefully curated to provide a mix of booster packs, exclusive promo cards, and a durable, often beautifully designed storage tin or box. This makes them a complete package that offers both the excitement of opening new cards and the practicality of card storage, all wrapped in one attractive product.

2. **Exclusive and Limited-Edition Items**: Many collector's boxes and tins include items that are not available in standard *Yu-Gi-Oh!* products. These exclusive promo cards and unique tins add a layer of rarity and collectibility, making them highly desirable for fans who want something special in their collection.

3. **Boosts Collection and Gameplay**: For players looking to expand their deck or build new strategies, the booster packs in-

cluded in these sets are an excellent way to add new cards to their collection. Promo cards included in these sets often feature powerful or meta-relevant monsters, making them useful for competitive play as well as casual duels.

4. **Beautiful and Functional Packaging**: The collectible tins and boxes are not just for looks—many players use them to store their cards and decks securely. The designs often feature iconic characters or monsters from the *Yu-Gi-Oh!* universe, adding aesthetic appeal to a player's collection.

5. **Memorable Gift for Fans of All Ages**: Whether the recipient is a casual player, a long-time fan, or a serious collector, these sets are memorable gifts that offer a bit of everything. The combination of cards, packs, and exclusive items makes them a well-rounded and thoughtful gift option.

Popular Collector's Boxes and Tins from Recent Years

In recent years, Konami has released several collector's boxes and tins that have become fan favorites. These sets feature exclusive content, rare cards, and beautifully designed tins that appeal to both players and collectors. Below, we'll highlight some of the most popular and sought-after collector's boxes and tins from recent releases.

1. 2022 Tin of the Pharaoh's Gods

One of the most celebrated collector's tins in recent years, the *2022 Tin of the Pharaoh's Gods* pays homage to the legendary Egyptian God cards—*Slifer the Sky Dragon*, *Obelisk the Tormentor*, and *The Winged Dragon of Ra*. This tin is part of the *Mega Tin* series and includes several exclusive cards and booster packs from recent sets.

- **What's Inside**:
  - Three *Mega Packs*, each containing a mix of cards from recent sets.

- ◦ Exclusive promo cards, including alternate artwork versions of iconic monsters like *Blue-Eyes White Dragon* and *Dark Magician Girl*.
  - ◦ A beautifully designed tin featuring Egyptian-themed artwork, ideal for storing cards or displaying on a shelf.
- **Why It's Popular**: The *2022 Tin of the Pharaoh's Gods* is highly sought after because of its connection to the legendary Egyptian God cards, as well as the inclusion of iconic monsters like *Blue-Eyes* and *Dark Magician*. The stunning artwork on the tin itself makes it a must-have for collectors, and the inclusion of *Mega Packs* provides plenty of opportunities to pull rare and valuable cards.

2. 2023 Tin of Dueling Legends

The *2023 Tin of Dueling Legends* is another standout release, featuring alternate artwork versions of beloved monsters and characters from the original *Yu-Gi-Oh!* anime. This tin celebrates classic duels and characters while offering new booster packs and exclusive promo cards.

- **What's Inside**:
  - ◦ Three *Mega Packs* featuring cards from sets like *Duelist Nexus* and *Photon Hypernova*.
  - ◦ Exclusive promo cards, including alternate artwork of fan-favorite monsters like *Red-Eyes Black Dragon* and *Dark Magician*.
  - ◦ A collector's tin designed with detailed artwork that highlights some of the most iconic moments and monsters from the *Yu-Gi-Oh!* anime.
- **Why It's Popular**: This tin appeals to both nostalgic fans of the original anime and players who are looking to expand their collection with modern cards. The inclusion of alternate artwork for beloved monsters and the *Mega Packs* that offer exciting pulls make this a great gift for both casual and competitive players.

3. Maximum Gold: El Dorado Collector's Box (2021)

Maximum Gold: El Dorado is a collector's box that focuses on providing players with premium gold-rare versions of some of the most iconic and powerful cards in the *Yu-Gi-Oh!* universe. The gold-bordered cards in this set are visually stunning, making them highly sought after by collectors.

- **What's Inside**:
    - Four *Maximum Gold: El Dorado* booster packs, each containing several gold rare cards.
    - Premium gold-rare versions of popular cards like *Accesscode Talker*, *Red-Eyes Black Dragon*, and *Blue-Eyes White Dragon*.
    - High-quality packaging that protects the cards and adds to the collectible appeal.
- **Why It's Popular**: The *Maximum Gold: El Dorado* collector's box is perfect for fans who value the aesthetic of their collection. The gold-bordered cards are not only beautiful but also include some of the most powerful cards in the game, making this set appealing to both collectors and players.

4. Legendary Collection: Kaiba (2018)

For fans of *Seto Kaiba* and his signature *Blue-Eyes White Dragon* deck, the *Legendary Collection: Kaiba* collector's box is a dream come true. This set celebrates the infamous duelist with exclusive cards and booster packs designed around Kaiba's iconic monsters and strategies.

- **What's Inside**:
    - Three *Legendary Collection* booster packs, each containing cards that support *Blue-Eyes* and other Kaiba-centric strategies.
    - Promo cards, including powerful reprints like *The King of D.* and *Destruction Dragon*.

- A *Kaiba*-themed game board that features artwork of Kaiba's most famous monsters, making it both a collectible item and a functional playmat.
- **Why It's Popular**: The *Legendary Collection: Kaiba* is perfect for fans of the original anime who want to recreate Kaiba's legendary deck or collect rare *Blue-Eyes* cards. The inclusion of a functional game board and powerful cards makes this set appealing to both collectors and competitive players.

5. Yu-Gi-Oh! Speed Duel GX: Duel Academy Box (2022)

The *Speed Duel GX: Duel Academy Box* focuses on the *Yu-Gi-Oh! GX* era and provides players with pre-built decks and cards designed for the Speed Duel format. This set is perfect for casual players who want to experience the *GX* series while enjoying fast-paced duels with simplified rules.

- **What's Inside**:
    - Eight pre-built Speed Duel decks, each representing a character from the *Yu-Gi-Oh! GX* anime.
    - Promo cards exclusive to the set, featuring *Elemental HERO* monsters and other *GX* archetypes.
    - A collector's box designed to hold all the decks and accessories.
- **Why It's Popular**: This set is perfect for fans of the *Yu-Gi-Oh! GX* series and those who enjoy the Speed Duel format. The pre-built decks allow players to jump straight into the action, and the inclusion of promo cards adds collectible value to the set.

How to Choose the Perfect Collector's Box or Tin

When selecting a collector's box or tin as a gift, consider the recipient's preferences and playstyle. Here are some tips to help you choose the perfect set:

1. **For Nostalgic Fans**: If the recipient is a long-time fan who grew up watching the original *Yu-Gi-Oh!* series, sets like the *2023 Tin of Dueling Legends* or the *Legendary Collection: Kaiba* will appeal to their sense of nostalgia. These sets feature characters and monsters from the classic anime and include powerful cards that pay homage to the show's most iconic moments.

2. **For Competitive Players**: For competitive players looking to expand their collection with useful cards, tins like the *2022 Tin of the Pharaoh's Gods* or *Maximum Gold: El Dorado* offer high-value cards that can be used in modern decks. These tins also include *Mega Packs* or gold-rare cards, providing plenty of options for deck-building.

3. **For Collectors**: If the recipient enjoys collecting rare and exclusive items, choose a set that includes promo cards or limited-edition items, such as the *Maximum Gold: El Dorado* or the *Legendary Collection: Kaiba*. These sets feature beautiful artwork and rare cards that will enhance any collector's display.

4. **For Casual Players**: For those who enjoy the game but are not heavily involved in competitive play, sets like the *Speed Duel GX: Duel Academy Box* offer fun, pre-built decks that can be enjoyed casually with friends. These sets are easy to jump into and provide a great introduction to the *Yu-Gi-Oh!* universe.

Conclusion

Collector's boxes and tins offer a unique and exciting way to experience the *Yu-Gi-Oh!* TCG, combining the thrill of opening booster packs with the value of exclusive promo cards and durable storage solutions. Whether you're buying for a competitive player, a nostalgic fan, or a dedicated collector, these sets provide a comprehensive package that brings joy and excitement to any *Yu-Gi-Oh!* fan. With beautifully designed tins, rare cards, and plenty of booster packs to explore, collector's boxes and tins are the perfect gift for fans of all ages.

Chapter 9: Yu-Gi-Oh! Video Games

The *Yu-Gi-Oh!* franchise extends far beyond the physical trading card game (TCG), with video games that allow fans to enjoy the world of dueling in exciting new ways. From console and PC games that faithfully recreate the TCG experience to mobile apps that offer fast-paced duels on the go, *Yu-Gi-Oh!* video games provide a digital playground for fans to hone their skills, experiment with new decks, and engage with players from around the world. These games offer a convenient and immersive way to experience the *Yu-Gi-Oh!* universe without the need for physical cards or a nearby opponent.

In this chapter, we'll explore the diverse range of *Yu-Gi-Oh!* video games available across different platforms, discuss which games are best suited for various types of players, and provide an overview of the most popular titles. Whether you're gifting a console gamer, a PC enthusiast, or a mobile player, there's a *Yu-Gi-Oh!* game that offers something for every fan.

The Appeal of Yu-Gi-Oh! Video Games

For many fans, *Yu-Gi-Oh!* video games offer a way to enjoy the strategy and excitement of dueling without the need for a physical deck or an in-person opponent. These games provide access to thousands of cards, allowing players to build decks, test new strategies, and compete with other duelists online. The digital format also allows for faster gameplay, automated rules enforcement, and unique game modes that aren't possible in the physical card game.

Here's why *Yu-Gi-Oh!* video games are so appealing:

1. **Accessibility**: Video games make the *Yu-Gi-Oh!* TCG more accessible to players who may not have access to physical cards or nearby opponents. Online matchmaking allows players to duel opponents from around the world, ensuring there's always someone to play against.

2. **Deck Building and Experimentation**: With a vast library of cards available in most games, players can experiment with different deck builds, try out new strategies, and refine their playstyle. Video games offer a risk-free environment to test new ideas before committing to a physical deck.

3. **Fast-Paced Gameplay**: The digital format allows for faster duels, with automated rules enforcement and streamlined gameplay mechanics. This makes it easier for players to focus on strategy and enjoy more matches in a shorter period of time.

4. **Unique Game Modes**: Many *Yu-Gi-Oh!* video games feature special game modes that aren't possible in the physical TCG, such as story-driven campaigns, puzzle challenges, or unique formats. These modes offer a fresh and engaging way to experience the game.

5. **Nostalgia and Storytelling**: Some *Yu-Gi-Oh!* video games offer story modes that allow players to relive key moments from the anime or manga. For fans of the original series, these games provide a nostalgic journey through the iconic duels and characters they grew up with.

Console and PC Yu-Gi-Oh! Games: The Ultimate Digital Dueling Experience

Console and PC games offer a robust, immersive experience for *Yu-Gi-Oh!* fans who want to dive deep into the world of digital dueling. These games often feature stunning graphics, in-depth story modes, and access to a vast library of cards, allowing players to fully explore the strategic depth of the TCG. With competitive online modes, ranked duels, and multiplayer tournaments, console and PC *Yu-Gi-Oh!* games provide a competitive playground for serious duelists.

Below are some of the most popular console and PC *Yu-Gi-Oh!* games, each offering a unique experience for different types of players:

1. **Yu-Gi-Oh! Master Duel (2022)**

Yu-Gi-Oh! Master Duel is one of the most recent and comprehensive *Yu-Gi-Oh!* games available, offering an authentic TCG experience with thousands of cards to collect and use in duels. Available on multiple platforms, including PC, PlayStation, Xbox, and Nintendo Switch, *Master Duel* is designed for competitive play and features ranked duels, tournaments, and regular updates that reflect the current TCG metagame.

- **Key Features**:
    - Access to over 10,000 cards, including classic and modern sets.
    - Competitive ranked duels and tournaments with global leaderboards.
    - Stunning 3D graphics and animations that bring the cards and monsters to life.
    - A solo mode with in-depth tutorials and story-driven campaigns that explore the lore behind various archetypes.
- **Who It's For**:
    - **Competitive Players**: *Master Duel* is ideal for players who want to engage in high-level competitive duels with opponents from around the world. The game's ranked ladder and tournament system provide a structured environment for testing one's skills.
    - **Experienced Duelists**: With access to the full range of cards and strategies, this game is perfect for advanced players who are familiar with the TCG and want to build complex, meta-relevant decks.
- **Why It's Popular**: *Master Duel* offers one of the most complete and polished *Yu-Gi-Oh!* experiences available, with regular updates that keep the game fresh and aligned with the official TCG. The ability to compete in ranked duels, participate in events, and

customize decks makes this game a favorite among serious duelists.

2. Yu-Gi-Oh! Legacy of the Duelist: Link Evolution (2019)

Yu-Gi-Oh! Legacy of the Duelist: Link Evolution is a fan-favorite title that allows players to relive iconic moments from the *Yu-Gi-Oh!* anime and build decks from across all generations of the TCG. Available on Nintendo Switch, PlayStation 4, Xbox One, and PC, this game includes content from the original series through *Yu-Gi-Oh! VRAINS*, making it a nostalgic journey through the franchise's history.

- **Key Features**:
    - Story mode that lets players reenact key duels from the anime, spanning multiple series.
    - Over 10,000 cards to collect and build decks with, including *Link* monsters and modern archetypes.
    - Local and online multiplayer modes, allowing players to duel friends or challenge others online.
    - Includes all TCG mechanics, including Fusion, Synchro, Xyz, and Link Summoning.
- **Who It's For**:
    - **Nostalgic Fans**: This game is perfect for fans who grew up watching the anime and want to relive their favorite duels. The story mode allows players to take control of characters like Yugi, Kaiba, and Jaden and reenact their most memorable matches.
    - **Casual and Competitive Players**: With a balance between casual story-driven gameplay and competitive online dueling, this game appeals to both casual fans and players who want to test their decks against real opponents.
- **Why It's Popular**: The combination of nostalgia, comprehensive card collection, and competitive play makes *Legacy of the Duelist: Link Evolution* a versatile game that appeals to a broad

audience. Fans of all generations of the anime will enjoy the opportunity to relive key moments while also building decks with modern strategies.

3. Yu-Gi-Oh! Duel Links (2017)

Yu-Gi-Oh! Duel Links is a popular mobile and PC game that offers a streamlined version of the *Yu-Gi-Oh!* TCG, designed for fast-paced, on-the-go dueling. With simplified rules, smaller decks, and shorter duels, *Duel Links* is ideal for players who want a quick, engaging *Yu-Gi-Oh!* experience without the complexity of the full TCG.

- **Key Features**:
  - 3D battle animations and iconic character voices from the anime.
  - Fast-paced duels with simplified rules, using 3 Monster Zones and 3 Spell/Trap Zones.
  - A huge roster of characters from across the *Yu-Gi-Oh!* anime, each with unique abilities and skills.
  - Regular in-game events, tournaments, and new card releases that keep the game fresh.
- **Who It's For**:
  - **Mobile Players**: *Duel Links* is perfect for players who want to enjoy *Yu-Gi-Oh!* on the go. Its mobile-friendly interface and shorter duels make it ideal for quick matches during a break or while commuting.
  - **Casual Fans**: The simplified gameplay makes this game accessible to casual players who may not be familiar with the full complexity of the TCG. The inclusion of anime characters and their unique skills adds an extra layer of fun for fans of the show.
- **Why It's Popular**: *Duel Links* is one of the most accessible *Yu-Gi-Oh!* games available, with millions of players around the world. The game's fast-paced duels, frequent updates, and nostal-

gic anime content make it a favorite for both casual players and fans of the anime.

4. Yu-Gi-Oh! Rush Duel: Dawn of the Battle Royale!! (2021)

Yu-Gi-Oh! Rush Duel: Dawn of the Battle Royale!! introduces the *Rush Duel* format, a new style of gameplay that originated in Japan and is aimed at younger or more casual players. Available on the Nintendo Switch, this game offers a fun, fast-paced dueling experience with simplified mechanics and an emphasis on quick decision-making.

- **Key Features**:
  - Rush Duel format with simplified rules, allowing players to draw multiple cards per turn and summon as many monsters as they want.
  - Story mode that follows characters from the *Yu-Gi-Oh! SEVENS* anime.
  - Unique card collection and deck-building options that reflect the *Rush Duel* format.
- **Who It's For**:
  - **Younger Players**: The simplified rules and fast-paced gameplay make this game perfect for younger players or those new to *Yu-Gi-Oh!*.
  - **Fans of the Rush Duel Format**: Players who enjoy the *Rush Duel* format, which is currently popular in Japan, will appreciate this game's focus on rapid, action-packed duels.
- **Why It's Popular**: *Rush Duel: Dawn of the Battle Royale!!* is a fun and engaging game for fans of the *Rush Duel* format. Its simple mechanics and fast gameplay make it accessible to younger players, while its story mode and character-driven content provide plenty of entertainment for fans of the *Yu-Gi-Oh! SEVENS* anime.

Mobile Yu-Gi-Oh! Games: Dueling on the Go

For fans who prefer to duel on their mobile devices, *Yu-Gi-Oh!* offers a range of mobile games that cater to different playstyles and preferences. These games are perfect for casual players who want to enjoy quick matches on the go, as well as competitive players who seek a mobile dueling experience.

Here are two of the most popular mobile *Yu-Gi-Oh!* games:

1. Yu-Gi-Oh! Duel Links (2017)

As mentioned earlier, *Duel Links* is one of the most popular mobile *Yu-Gi-Oh!* games, with a streamlined version of the TCG that allows for fast-paced duels and mobile-friendly mechanics. It offers regular in-game events, character unlocks, and competitive tournaments, making it a staple for mobile players.

- **Why It's Popular**: Its combination of quick, accessible duels and deep strategy keeps players engaged for the long term. Frequent updates and events ensure that there's always something new to enjoy.

2. Yu-Gi-Oh! Cross Duel (2022)

Yu-Gi-Oh! Cross Duel introduces a fresh take on the *Yu-Gi-Oh!* TCG by offering a four-player battle format where duelists compete simultaneously in a fast-paced and strategic environment. The game is available on mobile platforms and provides a unique twist for fans looking for something different from traditional one-on-one duels.

- **Key Features**:
    - Four-player free-for-all duels, with players battling for control over multiple zones.
    - Simple mechanics designed for quick matches.
    - Regular events, challenges, and unlockable rewards.
- **Who It's For**:

- ○ **Casual Mobile Players**: This game is designed for quick and casual mobile duels, with a unique multiplayer experience that stands out from other *Yu-Gi-Oh!* games.
  - ○ **Fans of Multiplayer Strategy**: The four-player format makes this game ideal for players who enjoy strategic battles with multiple opponents.
- **Why It's Popular**: *Cross Duel* offers a fresh approach to the *Yu-Gi-Oh!* experience, with a focus on multiplayer duels and simplified mechanics. It's perfect for players who want a more casual, yet strategic, mobile experience.

How to Choose the Best Yu-Gi-Oh! Video Game for Different Players

When selecting a *Yu-Gi-Oh!* video game as a gift, consider the recipient's preferences and gaming habits. Here are some tips to help you choose the best game based on the player's style:

1. **For Competitive Players**: If the recipient enjoys building meta-relevant decks and competing against players from around the world, *Yu-Gi-Oh! Master Duel* is the perfect choice. Its ranked duels and extensive card collection make it ideal for serious duelists.
2. **For Casual Players or Fans of the Anime**: If the recipient enjoys the anime and wants to relive key moments from the series, *Yu-Gi-Oh! Legacy of the Duelist: Link Evolution* is a great option. The story mode, combined with online dueling, offers a balanced experience for both casual and competitive players.
3. **For Younger or New Players**: For younger players or those new to *Yu-Gi-Oh!*, *Yu-Gi-Oh! Rush Duel: Dawn of the Battle Royale!!* is a fun and accessible game that introduces the Rush Duel format in an engaging and simple way.
4. **For Mobile Gamers**: If the recipient prefers mobile gaming, *Yu-Gi-Oh! Duel Links* is the best choice for quick, on-the-go dueling.

Its streamlined gameplay and large player base make it a favorite among mobile players.

Conclusion

Yu-Gi-Oh! video games offer a wide range of experiences for fans of all types, whether they're competitive duelists, casual players, or long-time fans of the anime. From console and PC games that provide a deep and immersive TCG experience to mobile games designed for quick, fast-paced dueling, there's a *Yu-Gi-Oh!* game for every type of player. These video games are perfect gifts for fans who want to enjoy the excitement of dueling in the digital realm, offering endless hours of strategic gameplay and fun.

Chapter 10: Anime and Manga Merchandise

While the *Yu-Gi-Oh!* Trading Card Game (TCG) is the cornerstone of the franchise, the *Yu-Gi-Oh!* anime and manga have had a profound impact on fans around the world. Many players were first introduced to the *Yu-Gi-Oh!* universe through the anime or manga, and these media continue to be beloved by fans long after their original release. The captivating storylines, iconic duels, and memorable characters have left an indelible mark on pop culture, making anime and manga merchandise an appealing gift option for fans who enjoy immersing themselves in the broader *Yu-Gi-Oh!* universe.

In this chapter, we will explore a range of *Yu-Gi-Oh!* anime and manga-themed merchandise, from complete DVD sets and manga collections to figurines, posters, and more. Whether you're shopping for a fan of the original series or someone who has followed the franchise through its various spin-offs, there are plenty of ways to celebrate their love for the *Yu-Gi-Oh!* world beyond the card game.

The Appeal of Yu-Gi-Oh! Anime and Manga Merchandise

For many fans, the *Yu-Gi-Oh!* anime and manga were their first introduction to the franchise, and these media remain integral to the *Yu-Gi-Oh!* experience. The stories told in the anime and manga bring the card game to life, with characters like *Yugi*, *Kaiba*, *Joey*, and *Atem* engaging in high-stakes duels that have become iconic. These adventures have been adapted into numerous series, movies, and spin-offs, creating a wealth of content that spans decades.

Here's why *Yu-Gi-Oh!* anime and manga merchandise makes such an appealing gift:

1. **Nostalgia and Emotional Connection**: For fans who grew up watching the *Yu-Gi-Oh!* anime or reading the manga, the series holds deep emotional resonance. Revisiting favorite episodes, characters, and duels through merchandise allows fans to reconnect with the stories that first sparked their love for the franchise.

2. **Iconic Characters and Monsters**: The *Yu-Gi-Oh!* anime and manga introduced some of the most iconic characters and monsters in popular culture. From *Yugi Mutou* and *Seto Kaiba* to *Dark Magician* and *Blue-Eyes White Dragon*, these characters have become symbols of the franchise, and merchandise that celebrates them is always in demand.

3. **Collectibility**: Many fans of the *Yu-Gi-Oh!* anime and manga are also collectors, and merchandise related to these media offers a way to build a tangible collection of favorite characters, scenes, and moments from the series.

4. **Expanding the Universe**: Anime and manga merchandise allows fans to immerse themselves in the *Yu-Gi-Oh!* universe beyond the card game. Whether it's owning a physical collection of manga volumes or decorating their space with posters and figurines, fans can bring their favorite stories to life in new and exciting ways.

Yu-Gi-Oh! DVD and Blu-ray Collections

For fans who want to relive the *Yu-Gi-Oh!* anime experience, DVD and Blu-ray collections are the perfect way to enjoy the series from the beginning. The *Yu-Gi-Oh!* anime spans multiple generations, with different series covering different eras, duels, and characters. These collections offer a comprehensive way to watch favorite episodes, revisit key duels, or introduce new fans to the world of *Yu-Gi-Oh!*.

Why DVD and Blu-ray Collections Make a Great Gift

- **Nostalgic Experience**: Watching the *Yu-Gi-Oh!* anime offers a nostalgic trip back to the duels that defined the series. For long-time fans, owning a complete set of DVDs or Blu-rays allows them to relive the moments they loved growing up.

- **Comprehensive Viewing**: Complete collections provide access to every episode of a series, from the original *Yu-Gi-Oh!* to *Yu-Gi-Oh! GX*, *Yu-Gi-Oh! 5D's*, and beyond. These sets often include bonus features such as interviews, behind-the-scenes content, and commentary.

- **Convenience**: Having a physical collection of the anime makes it easy to watch favorite episodes anytime without relying on streaming services, ensuring that the series is always accessible.

Popular Yu-Gi-Oh! DVD and Blu-ray Sets

1. **Yu-Gi-Oh! Classic Complete Series Box Set**: This set includes all episodes from the original *Yu-Gi-Oh!* series, following the story of *Yugi Mutou*, his friends, and their battles with powerful opponents like *Seto Kaiba* and *Maximillion Pegasus*. This is the perfect gift for fans who want to relive the entire story from the Duelist Kingdom arc to the final battle against *Atem* in the Ceremonial Duel.

2. **Yu-Gi-Oh! GX Complete Series**: *Yu-Gi-Oh! GX* takes place in the Duel Academy, focusing on the adventures of *Jaden Yuki* and his friends. The *GX* series introduces new mechanics like Fusion Summoning and brings new archetypes to the forefront. This complete set is great for fans of the *GX* era or those who want to explore the *Yu-Gi-Oh!* universe beyond the original series.

3. **Yu-Gi-Oh! The Dark Side of Dimensions Blu-ray**: For fans who loved the original series, this movie continues the story of *Yugi* and *Kaiba* as they face new challenges after the events of the main series. This Blu-ray release offers stunning animation and an epic new duel, making it a great addition to any fan's collection.

Yu-Gi-Oh! Manga Collections

The *Yu-Gi-Oh!* manga, created by Kazuki Takahashi, predates the anime and serves as the foundation of the entire franchise. While the manga's storyline largely mirrors the anime, it offers a darker, more detailed exploration of the characters, their motivations, and the mythology behind the *Millennium Items*. Collecting the *Yu-Gi-Oh!* manga is a must for fans who want to dive deeper into the lore or experience the original story as it was intended.

Why Manga Collections Make a Great Gift

- **Original Storytelling**: The manga provides the most authentic version of the *Yu-Gi-Oh!* story, with additional context and character development that may not be fully explored in the anime.
- **Beautiful Artwork**: Kazuki Takahashi's artwork brings the characters and duels to life in a unique way, with dramatic visuals that capture the intensity of each duel.
- **Collector's Appeal**: Owning a full set of the *Yu-Gi-Oh!* manga is a point of pride for collectors, and special box sets or hardcover editions make for stunning display pieces in any fan's collection.

Popular Yu-Gi-Oh! Manga Sets

1. **Yu-Gi-Oh! 3-in-1 Edition**: This manga series compiles three volumes of the original *Yu-Gi-Oh!* manga into one book, making it an affordable and space-saving way to collect the entire series. The 3-in-1 edition covers the entire journey of *Yugi Mutou*, from his first encounter with the *Millennium Puzzle* to his final duel against *Atem*.

2. **Yu-Gi-Oh! Millennium World**: This manga series focuses on the final arc of the original story, where *Yugi* travels to ancient Egypt to uncover the secrets of *Atem*'s past. For fans who want to explore the origins of the *Millennium Items* and witness the epic conclusion to the *Yu-Gi-Oh!* saga, this collection is a must-have.

3. **Yu-Gi-Oh! R Manga Series**: *Yu-Gi-Oh! R* is a spin-off manga that takes place between the Battle City arc and the *Millennium World* arc of the original series. It offers a new storyline involving *Yugi* and his friends as they battle against a new villain. This series is great for fans who want to explore an alternate take on the *Yu-Gi-Oh!* universe.

Figurines and Statues: Bring Your Favorite Characters to Life

For fans who love collecting physical representations of their favorite characters, *Yu-Gi-Oh!* figurines and statues are a fantastic gift option. These highly detailed models capture iconic characters and monsters in dynamic poses, making them perfect for display in any fan's collection. Whether it's a miniature version of *Yugi Mutou* or a towering statue of *Blue-Eyes White Dragon*, these collectibles allow fans to bring their favorite duels to life.

Why Figurines and Statues Make a Great Gift

- **Highly Detailed**: Figurines and statues are often crafted with meticulous attention to detail, capturing the likeness of characters and monsters with impressive accuracy.
- **Display Value**: These collectibles are designed for display, allowing fans to create visually stunning showcases of their favorite characters. For serious collectors, limited-edition statues can become the centerpiece of their collection.
- **Wide Range of Characters**: From *Yugi Mutou* and *Seto Kaiba* to monsters like *Dark Magician* and *Red-Eyes Black Dragon*, there are figurines and statues available for nearly every iconic character in the series.

Popular Yu-Gi-Oh! Figurines and Statues

1. **Kotobukiya Dark Magician 1/7 Scale Statue**: This beautifully crafted statue of *Dark Magician* is a collector's dream. It features the iconic spellcaster in a dynamic casting pose, complete with a detailed base and vibrant colors. For fans of *Yugi*'s signature monster, this statue is an impressive and eye-catching display piece.
2. **Figma Yami Yugi Action Figure**: The *Figma* action figure line offers a poseable version of *Yami Yugi*, allowing fans to recreate famous scenes from the anime. This figure comes with accessories

like the *Millennium Puzzle* and *Duel Disk*, making it a versatile and fun collectible.

3. **Banpresto Yu-Gi-Oh! Monsters Blue-Eyes White Dragon Figure**: For fans of *Seto Kaiba* and his iconic *Blue-Eyes White Dragon*, this detailed figure captures the majesty and power of the legendary monster. It's a must-have for fans who want to add a touch of *Kaiba Corp.* flair to their collection.

Posters, Wall Art, and Other Decor

For fans looking to bring their love for the *Yu-Gi-Oh!* anime and manga into their personal space, posters, wall art, and other decor items are the perfect solution. These items allow fans to decorate their rooms, gaming spaces, or offices with images of their favorite characters, monsters, and duels.

Why Posters and Wall Art Make a Great Gift

- **Affordable and Versatile**: Posters and wall art are budget-friendly gifts that offer a lot of visual impact. They can be easily swapped out, making them versatile decor options for fans who like to change up their space.
- **Iconic Imagery**: Posters featuring characters like *Yugi, Kaiba, Joey,* and iconic monsters like *Dark Magician* or *Blue-Eyes White Dragon* are perfect for fans who want to showcase their favorite parts of the series.
- **Personalized Spaces**: Wall art allows fans to personalize their space with visuals that reflect their passion for the *Yu-Gi-Oh!* franchise, creating an environment that inspires creativity and nostalgia.

Popular Yu-Gi-Oh! Posters and Wall Art

1. **Yu-Gi-Oh! Duel Monsters Poster Set**: This set includes several posters featuring artwork from the original *Yu-Gi-Oh!* series,

showcasing key duels and characters like *Yugi* and *Kaiba*. It's perfect for decorating a gaming room or bedroom.

2. **Millennium Puzzle Wall Art**: Fans of the *Millennium Puzzle* and its ancient Egyptian symbolism will love this art piece, which features the iconic puzzle as the centerpiece. It's a great gift for fans who appreciate the deeper lore of the series.

3. **Yu-Gi-Oh! Tapestries**: For something a bit more unique, tapestries featuring artwork of *Dark Magician*, *Blue-Eyes White Dragon*, or scenes from the anime make for dramatic wall decor. These tapestries are a creative way to display fandom while adding texture to a room.

Other Anime and Manga-Themed Merchandise
For fans who want to incorporate *Yu-Gi-Oh!* into their daily lives, there's a wealth of other merchandise options, including clothing, accessories, and practical items that feature designs from the anime and manga. These items are great for fans who want to wear their love for *Yu-Gi-Oh!* or incorporate it into their daily routines.

Popular Anime and Manga-Themed Merchandise

1. **Yu-Gi-Oh! Apparel**: T-shirts, hoodies, and hats featuring iconic characters and monsters are always a hit with fans. Designs featuring *Yugi*, *Kaiba*, *Dark Magician*, and *Blue-Eyes White Dragon* are particularly popular and make great casual gifts for fans of all ages.

2. **Yu-Gi-Oh! Mugs and Drinkware**: For a more practical gift, consider mugs or water bottles featuring *Yu-Gi-Oh!* designs. Fans can enjoy their morning coffee or tea with a mug that features their favorite duel monster or character.

3. **Millennium Puzzle Jewelry**: For fans of the ancient Egyptian themes in the series, jewelry such as *Millennium Puzzle* necklaces or rings are a subtle and stylish way to carry a piece of the *Yu-Gi-Oh!* world with them wherever they go.

Why Anime and Manga Merchandise Make Excellent Gifts

Anime and manga merchandise allows fans to connect with their favorite characters, stories, and moments from the *Yu-Gi-Oh!* franchise in tangible ways. Whether it's through a complete anime collection, a beautiful figurine, or a cozy hoodie featuring their favorite monster, these gifts offer a personal and meaningful way to celebrate their love for the series. With a wide range of products to choose from, there's something for every fan, from casual viewers to hardcore collectors.

Chapter 11: Custom Cards and Fan Art

For *Yu-Gi-Oh!* fans, the allure of a favorite character, monster, or duel goes beyond what can be found in the official merchandise. Personalized gifts like custom cards, fan art, and commissioned pieces offer a unique, thoughtful, and creative way to celebrate someone's love for the *Yu-Gi-Oh!* franchise. These gifts allow fans to own a one-of-a-kind piece of art that reflects their favorite aspects of the series, creating a personal connection that standard merchandise often cannot match. Whether it's a custom-designed card featuring an iconic monster with a twist, or a commissioned artwork capturing a memorable duel, these gifts can turn a fan's passion into something tangible and special.

In this chapter, we'll explore the world of custom cards, fan art, and personalized commissions, explaining why they make excellent gifts for *Yu-Gi-Oh!* enthusiasts. We'll also provide ideas on how to create or commission these items and offer suggestions for different types of fans, from those who love specific monsters to players who enjoy personalizing their decks.

The Appeal of Custom Cards and Fan Art

While official *Yu-Gi-Oh!* products are beloved by fans, custom cards and fan art bring a level of personalization that adds a deeper, more meaningful connection to the recipient's favorite aspects of the game, anime, or manga. Personalized artwork or custom cards based on a fan's favorite character or monster provide a creative and thoughtful touch, making these gifts stand out as unique and memorable.

Here's why custom cards and fan art are such appealing gift ideas:

1. **Personalized Connection** Custom cards and artwork can be tailored specifically to the recipient's favorite characters, monsters, or moments from the *Yu-Gi-Oh!* franchise. This personalized touch makes the gift feel special, as it reflects their personal tastes and fandom.

2. **Unique and One-of-a-Kind**: Unlike mass-produced merchandise, custom items are often one-of-a-kind, making them a truly unique gift. Fans can feel proud owning something that no one else has, whether it's a custom card designed just for them or a commissioned piece of art that reflects their love for a specific part of the franchise.

3. **Artistic Expression**: Fan art and custom cards allow artists to put their own creative spin on beloved characters, monsters, and duels. This artistic expression offers fans a new way to see their favorite elements of the series and makes for a visually stunning display piece.

4. **Perfect for Collectors**: For fans who are also collectors, owning a custom card or commissioned artwork is a special addition to their collection. These items are often displayed prominently, serving as a reminder of the fan's deep connection to the *Yu-Gi-Oh!* universe.

Custom Cards: Bringing Favorite Monsters to Life

Custom *Yu-Gi-Oh!* cards are one of the most creative ways to personalize a gift for a fan. These cards are typically designed based on existing monsters, characters, or spells from the *Yu-Gi-Oh!* TCG but with a unique twist. Artists and designers can create alternate artwork for the cards, add custom stats, or even design entirely new cards inspired by the recipient's personality or favorite archetypes.

Why Custom Cards Make a Great Gift

- **Personalization**: Custom cards can be tailored to reflect the recipient's favorite monsters, spells, or characters. For example, if the recipient loves *Dark Magician*, you could commission a custom card featuring alternate artwork of the iconic monster or even create a new spell card that complements the *Dark Magician* archetype.

- **Creativity and Fun**: Designing a custom card offers endless possibilities for creativity. You can alter the card's stats, change its effects, or even create a brand-new card that doesn't exist in the official TCG. This adds an element of fun, as the recipient can use their imagination to envision how the card fits into their favorite deck or duel.

- **Collector's Value**: Custom cards are often one-of-a-kind pieces that are meant for display rather than competitive play. For collectors, these cards hold a special place in their collection, representing a fusion of their love for the *Yu-Gi-Oh!* TCG and personal artistry.

Types of Custom Cards

1. **Alternate Art Cards**: These custom cards take existing *Yu-Gi-Oh!* cards and give them a new visual twist by featuring alternate artwork. For example, a custom *Blue-Eyes White Dragon* card might feature a stylized, hand-drawn version of the monster, or a *Dark Magician Girl* card could have a more detailed and dynamic pose than the original. These cards are popular among collectors who want to showcase their favorite monsters in a fresh, artistic way.

2. **Personalized Character Cards**: Another fun option is creating a custom card that reflects the personality of the recipient. You can design a new monster or spell card inspired by the recipient's interests or hobbies, giving the card custom stats and effects. For example, you could create a card called *"Duelist Champion [Name]"* with stats and abilities that reflect the recipient's skill as a player.

3. **Themed Deck Cards**: For fans of specific archetypes or deck themes, custom cards can be designed to expand their favorite decks in imaginative ways. For example, you could commission a series of cards that build on the *HERO* or *Elemental HERO*

archetype, adding new abilities or characters that fit within the theme. This is a great way to enhance the recipient's favorite deck while adding a personal touch.

Fan Art and Commissioned Pieces: Capturing Iconic Moments

Fan art is a beloved part of any fandom, and the *Yu-Gi-Oh!* community is no exception. Many talented artists create beautiful illustrations of iconic duels, characters, and monsters from the anime and manga, offering fans a chance to own unique pieces that celebrate their favorite aspects of the series. Commissioning artwork is also a fantastic way to create a truly personalized gift, as you can request specific scenes, character interactions, or monster depictions that are meaningful to the recipient.

Why Fan Art and Commissioned Pieces Make a Great Gift

- **Personalized Scenes**: Commissioning an artist to create a piece based on the recipient's favorite *Yu-Gi-Oh!* moment, character, or monster adds a deeply personal touch. For example, you could commission a piece depicting the final duel between *Yugi* and *Kaiba* or a custom portrait of the recipient's favorite monster.
- **Unique Artistic Style**: Fan art allows artists to reinterpret *Yu-Gi-Oh!* characters and duels in their own artistic style. This gives fans a fresh and unique perspective on their favorite characters, making the art stand out from official merchandise.
- **Display and Decoration**: Fan art is often designed to be displayed, making it perfect for framing and hanging in the recipient's home, office, or gaming room. High-quality prints or original paintings can transform a room into a tribute to the *Yu-Gi-Oh!* universe.

Types of Fan Art and Commissioned Pieces

1. **Character Portraits**: Commissioning a portrait of a favorite character, such as *Yugi*, *Kaiba*, *Joey*, or *Atem*, is a great way to create a personalized piece of art that the recipient can proudly display. These portraits can be done in a range of styles, from realistic to stylized, depending on the recipient's taste.

2. **Duel Scenes**: For fans who have a favorite duel or moment from the anime or manga, commissioning a scene that captures that moment is a special gift. For example, you could commission an artist to recreate the *Battle City* finals between *Yugi* and *Marik* or the iconic duel between *Kaiba* and *Pegasus*. This type of artwork is ideal for fans who love the strategy and drama of the series' most memorable duels.

3. **Monster Art**: For fans who are particularly drawn to the monsters of the *Yu-Gi-Oh!* universe, custom art of their favorite monsters—such as *Blue-Eyes White Dragon*, *Dark Magician*, *Exodia the Forbidden One*, or *Red-Eyes Black Dragon*—is a fantastic gift. Artists can create dynamic and detailed illustrations of these monsters in action, perfect for display.

4. **Crossover Art**: For fans who love multiple fandoms, crossover fan art can be a fun and creative way to blend the recipient's interests. You can commission a piece that combines *Yu-Gi-Oh!* with another favorite franchise, such as *Pokemon*, *Dragon Ball*, or *One Piece*. This adds an extra layer of personalization to the artwork and makes it a truly unique piece.

How to Commission Custom Cards and Fan Art

Commissioning custom cards or fan art requires working with artists who specialize in *Yu-Gi-Oh!* designs. Many talented artists are available on platforms like Etsy, DeviantArt, and social media, and you can browse their portfolios to find someone whose style matches what you're looking for. Here's how to commission a custom piece:

1. **Find an Artist**: Look for artists who specialize in *Yu-Gi-Oh!* fan art or custom card designs. You can find these artists on platforms like Etsy, Twitter, Instagram, or websites dedicated to fan art. Many artists will have portfolios where you can view their previous work and get a sense of their style.

2. **Communicate Your Vision**: Once you've chosen an artist, contact them with a clear idea of what you want. If you're commissioning a custom card, provide details about the card's name, stats, effects, and artwork. For fan art, specify the characters or scene you want depicted, as well as the style or medium you prefer (e.g., digital, traditional painting, etc.).

3. **Set Expectations**: Be sure to discuss pricing, timelines, and any revisions with the artist before they begin the project. Custom artwork can take time to complete, especially if it's a detailed piece, so make sure you're clear on when the artwork will be finished.

4. **Enjoy the Process**: One of the best parts of commissioning custom art is seeing your vision come to life. Many artists will provide updates along the way, allowing you to offer feedback and ensure the final piece is exactly what you envisioned.

Displaying Custom Cards and Fan Art

Once you've commissioned a custom card or piece of fan art, it's important to consider how to display it in a way that showcases its beauty and significance. Here are some ideas for displaying custom *Yu-Gi-Oh!* cards and artwork:

1. **Framing**: For fan art, framing the piece is an excellent way to protect and display it. Choose a frame that complements the artwork and enhances the overall aesthetic, and consider placing it in a prominent spot where the recipient can enjoy it every day.

2. **Card Display Cases**: Custom *Yu-Gi-Oh!* cards can be placed in protective card sleeves and displayed in acrylic or glass cases. These cases protect the card while allowing it to be showcased as a centerpiece in a collection.

3. **Shadow Boxes**: For a more creative display, consider using a shadow box to display a combination of custom cards and fan art. Shadow boxes provide a 3D display option and can hold multiple items, such as a custom card alongside a piece of fan art featuring the same monster or character.

4. **Digital Displays**: If the fan art is digital, consider creating a rotating digital frame that displays different pieces of commissioned art. This adds a modern touch and allows the recipient to enjoy multiple pieces without taking up wall space.

Why Custom Cards and Fan Art Make Excellent Gifts

Custom cards and fan art offer a personal and thoughtful way to celebrate a fan's love for the *Yu-Gi-Oh!* franchise. These gifts are one-of-a-kind, tailored to the recipient's favorite aspects of the series, and provide a unique expression of fandom that mass-produced merchandise simply can't replicate. Whether it's a custom card featuring alternate artwork or a commissioned piece of art that captures a beloved duel, these gifts are sure to be cherished and displayed with pride.

Chapter 12: Yu-Gi-Oh! Apparel and Fashion

For *Yu-Gi-Oh!* fans, expressing their love for the franchise isn't limited to collecting cards, watching the anime, or reading the manga—it can also extend to what they wear. *Yu-Gi-Oh!* apparel and fashion accessories allow fans to showcase their passion for the series in their everyday lives. From t-shirts and hoodies adorned with iconic monsters and characters to hats, jewelry, and other accessories featuring the *Millennium Items, Yu-Gi-Oh!* fashion items are a great way for fans to wear their fandom proudly.

In this chapter, we will explore a variety of *Yu-Gi-Oh!* apparel options and accessories, offering insights into the best pieces for different types of fans. Whether you're shopping for someone who loves bold character designs or a fan looking for subtle references to the franchise, there's a wide range of clothing and fashion accessories that make excellent wearable gifts. We'll also discuss where to find high-quality, officially licensed *Yu-Gi-Oh!* fashion items and how to incorporate these pieces into everyday wardrobes.

The Appeal of Yu-Gi-Oh! Apparel and Fashion Accessories

Apparel is one of the most versatile and accessible ways for fans to display their love for *Yu-Gi-Oh!* Fans of all ages can appreciate the opportunity to wear clothing that features their favorite characters, monsters, or symbols from the series. Fashion items such as t-shirts, hats, and hoodies provide a perfect blend of comfort and style while incorporating elements of the *Yu-Gi-Oh!* universe. Additionally, accessories like jewelry, socks, and bags can add a touch of *Yu-Gi-Oh!* flair to any outfit, allowing fans to subtly integrate their passion into their everyday look.

Here's why *Yu-Gi-Oh!* apparel and fashion accessories make such appealing gift options:

1. **Wearable Fandom**: Apparel allows fans to proudly display their love for *Yu-Gi-Oh!* in a way that is both practical and stylish.

Whether they're wearing a t-shirt featuring *Yugi* and *Kaiba* or a hoodie with *Blue-Eyes White Dragon*, fans can take their favorite characters and monsters with them wherever they go.

2. **Personal Expression**: Just as the *Yu-Gi-Oh!* TCG allows players to express their individual dueling style through their decks, apparel gives fans a chance to express their personal style while showcasing their fandom. With a wide range of designs and items to choose from, fans can find clothing and accessories that match their tastes, whether they prefer subtle nods to the series or bold, eye-catching graphics.

3. **Comfort and Practicality**: Many *Yu-Gi-Oh!* apparel items, such as t-shirts, hoodies, and hats, are designed for comfort and everyday wear. These pieces not only celebrate the franchise but also serve as practical additions to any wardrobe, making them excellent gifts that can be worn regularly.

4. **Gift Variety**: From clothing to accessories, there's a wide range of *Yu-Gi-Oh!* fashion items available, making it easy to find something for every fan. Whether it's a casual t-shirt for lounging at home, a statement hoodie for colder weather, or a stylish necklace featuring the *Millennium Puzzle*, these items offer diverse options for gift-giving.

Yu-Gi-Oh! Clothing: T-Shirts, Hoodies, and More

When it comes to *Yu-Gi-Oh!* fashion, t-shirts and hoodies are some of the most popular and versatile items. These clothing pieces often feature vibrant designs of iconic characters, monsters, or symbols from the franchise, making them perfect for casual wear. Whether the fan is drawn to the original series or one of the many spin-offs, there are plenty of designs that celebrate the heroes, villains, and legendary monsters that define *Yu-Gi-Oh!*.

Why T-Shirts and Hoodies Make Great Gifts

- **Comfortable and Stylish**: T-shirts and hoodies are wardrobe staples that can be worn year-round. A cozy hoodie featuring *Kaiba* and *Blue-Eyes White Dragon* or a lightweight t-shirt adorned with *Dark Magician* can be worn at home, to gaming events, or even casually in public, offering both comfort and style.
- **Bold Designs**: Many *Yu-Gi-Oh!* t-shirts and hoodies feature bold, colorful artwork of fan-favorite characters, monsters, or logos. These designs capture the essence of the series, making them visually striking pieces of clothing that stand out in any outfit.
- **Nostalgic Appeal**: For long-time fans, t-shirts and hoodies featuring characters from the original series (such as *Yugi Mutou*, *Kaiba*, or *Joey Wheeler*) tap into the nostalgia of the early days of the anime. Wearing these pieces allows fans to relive their favorite duels and moments from the series.

Popular Yu-Gi-Oh! Clothing Items

1. **Character T-Shirts**: T-shirts featuring iconic characters like *Yugi*, *Kaiba*, and *Joey* are among the most popular *Yu-Gi-Oh!* apparel items. These shirts often include dynamic artwork of the characters alongside their signature monsters, such as *Dark Magician* or *Blue-Eyes White Dragon*. Some designs even recreate famous duels from the anime, making them a hit with nostalgic fans.
2. **Monster-Themed Hoodies**: Hoodies featuring *Yu-Gi-Oh!* monsters like *Blue-Eyes White Dragon*, *Dark Magician*, *Red-Eyes Black Dragon*, and *Exodia the Forbidden One* are perfect for cooler weather. These designs often incorporate detailed artwork of the monsters in action, giving the clothing an epic, battle-ready aesthetic.

3. **Yu-Gi-Oh! Logo Shirts**: For fans who prefer a more minimalist approach, t-shirts featuring the official *Yu-Gi-Oh!* logo or the *Millennium Puzzle* symbol are subtle yet stylish ways to show their fandom. These shirts are perfect for everyday wear and can easily be paired with other casual clothing.

4. **Series-Specific Clothing**: Fans of different *Yu-Gi-Oh!* series, such as *Yu-Gi-Oh! GX*, *Yu-Gi-Oh! 5D's*, or *Yu-Gi-Oh! ZEXAL*, can find clothing that features characters and monsters from these spin-offs. T-shirts and hoodies featuring *Jaden Yuki* and the *Elemental HERO* monsters or *Yusei Fudo* and his *Synchro* monsters make great gifts for fans of these later series.

Yu-Gi-Oh! Hats and Accessories: Completing the Look

Beyond t-shirts and hoodies, *Yu-Gi-Oh!* fashion extends to a wide variety of accessories, including hats, beanies, socks, and jewelry. These items offer fans a more subtle way to incorporate their love for the franchise into their everyday outfits, adding a touch of *Yu-Gi-Oh!* flair to any look.

Why Hats and Accessories Make Great Gifts

- **Subtle Fandom**: Accessories like hats and jewelry provide a more understated way for fans to express their fandom. A hat featuring the *Millennium Eye* or a necklace shaped like the *Millennium Puzzle* adds a touch of *Yu-Gi-Oh!* to an outfit without being too bold or overpowering.

- **Variety and Versatility**: There's a wide range of *Yu-Gi-Oh!* accessories available, from practical items like hats and socks to more decorative pieces like necklaces and bracelets. This variety makes it easy to find the perfect accessory for any fan.

- **Complements Other Apparel**: Accessories are the perfect way to complete an outfit, whether it's adding a *Yu-Gi-Oh!* hat to a casual look or wearing a *Millennium Puzzle* necklace with a t-shirt featuring *Yugi* and *Kaiba*. These items allow fans to fully immerse themselves in the *Yu-Gi-Oh!* aesthetic.

Popular Yu-Gi-Oh! Hats and Accessories

1. **Millennium Puzzle Necklace**: One of the most iconic symbols from the *Yu-Gi-Oh!* franchise, the *Millennium Puzzle* is available in the form of a stylish necklace. This accessory is perfect for fans of *Yugi Mutou* and the ancient Egyptian themes of the series. The necklace is subtle enough to be worn daily but also holds significant meaning for fans of the show.

2. **Yu-Gi-Oh! Snapback Hats**: Hats featuring the *Yu-Gi-Oh!* logo or images of popular monsters like *Dark Magician* and *Blue-Eyes White Dragon* are a great way to add a touch of fandom to any casual outfit. Snapback hats are adjustable and come in a variety of designs, making them a versatile gift for fans of all ages.

3. **Millennium Item Jewelry Set**: For fans who love the lore behind the *Millennium Items*, a jewelry set that includes mini replicas of the *Millennium Puzzle*, *Millennium Eye*, *Millennium Ring*, and other items is a fantastic gift. These sets often come with necklaces or bracelets that feature detailed designs of the items, allowing fans to wear their favorite symbols from the series.

4. **Yu-Gi-Oh! Socks**: Socks featuring designs of iconic monsters like *Exodia* or *Dark Magician Girl* are fun, practical gifts that add a playful touch to any fan's wardrobe. These socks are often decorated with vibrant colors and detailed artwork, making them a quirky yet stylish choice for any *Yu-Gi-Oh!* enthusiast.

Yu-Gi-Oh! Backpacks and Bags: Carrying Fandom with Style

For fans who want to take their love for *Yu-Gi-Oh!* on the go, backpacks and bags featuring designs from the series offer both functionality and fandom. These items are perfect for carrying cards, decks, or everyday essentials while showcasing favorite characters and monsters.

Why Backpacks and Bags Make Great Gifts

- **Practical and Stylish**: Backpacks and bags are practical gifts that serve a functional purpose while also featuring stylish *Yu-Gi-Oh!* designs. Fans can use them to carry school supplies, gaming accessories, or personal items while displaying their love for the series.
- **Ideal for Tournaments and Events**: For competitive players who attend *Yu-Gi-Oh!* tournaments or local events, a stylish backpack is a great way to carry their decks, playmats, and other gaming supplies. These bags often feature padded compartments to protect cards and accessories.
- **Unique Designs**: Many *Yu-Gi-Oh!* backpacks and bags feature bold, colorful artwork of characters, monsters, or logos, making them visually striking and perfect for fans who want to stand out.

Popular Yu-Gi-Oh! Backpacks and Bags

1. **Dark Magician Girl Backpack**: This backpack features vibrant artwork of *Dark Magician Girl*, one of the most popular monsters in the franchise. The bag's design is playful and colorful, making it a great accessory for fans of all ages.
2. **Yu-Gi-Oh! Duel Disk Messenger Bag**: Inspired by the iconic *Duel Disk* from the anime, this messenger bag is designed to look like the device used by duelists to play their cards in the series. It's a perfect gift for fans who want a unique and practical bag

that celebrates one of the most recognizable pieces of *Yu-Gi-Oh!* equipment.

3. **Millennium Puzzle Tote Bag**: For fans of the *Millennium Items*, a tote bag featuring the *Millennium Puzzle* symbol is a stylish and subtle way to carry personal items while showcasing their love for the series. This bag is perfect for casual outings or carrying light supplies.

Where to Find Yu-Gi-Oh! Apparel and Fashion Accessories

When shopping for *Yu-Gi-Oh!* apparel and accessories, it's important to look for high-quality, officially licensed merchandise to ensure the designs are accurate and the materials are durable. Here are some of the best places to find *Yu-Gi-Oh!* fashion items:

1. **Official Yu-Gi-Oh! Store**: The official *Yu-Gi-Oh!* online store often carries a range of apparel and accessories, including t-shirts, hoodies, hats, and jewelry. These items are officially licensed, ensuring high quality and authentic designs.
2. **Etsy**: For unique, handmade *Yu-Gi-Oh!* apparel and accessories, Etsy is a great platform. Many independent artists and designers create custom clothing, hats, and jewelry inspired by the franchise. These items are often one-of-a-kind and offer a more personalized touch.
3. **Hot Topic**: Hot Topic is a popular retailer that often carries anime-themed apparel, including *Yu-Gi-Oh!* t-shirts, hoodies, and accessories. Their selection frequently features bold designs that appeal to younger fans and those who love statement clothing.
4. **Amazon**: Amazon offers a wide selection of *Yu-Gi-Oh!* clothing and accessories, including officially licensed merchandise. This is a convenient option for finding t-shirts, hats, and bags, with customer reviews to help ensure the quality of the products.

Why Yu-Gi-Oh! Apparel and Fashion Accessories Make Excellent Gifts

Yu-Gi-Oh! apparel and fashion accessories are a fun and practical way for fans to express their love for the franchise in their everyday lives. From bold t-shirts and hoodies to subtle jewelry and hats, these items offer a wide range of options for fans who want to incorporate *Yu-Gi-Oh!* into their personal style. Whether you're shopping for a casual fan or a dedicated collector, apparel and accessories make thoughtful and wearable gifts that can be enjoyed year-round.

Chapter 13: Yu-Gi-Oh! Themed Board Games

While the *Yu-Gi-Oh!* Trading Card Game (TCG) remains the heart of the franchise, there are also numerous board games and card-based spin-offs that offer fans alternative ways to experience the *Yu-Gi-Oh!* universe. These games provide new and exciting ways to engage with the franchise's characters, monsters, and mechanics, while offering a break from the traditional TCG. Whether you're a long-time fan of the card game or someone looking to explore new types of gameplay, *Yu-Gi-Oh!* themed board games offer fun, strategic challenges that can be enjoyed by both casual and competitive players alike.

In this chapter, we'll delve into the world of *Yu-Gi-Oh!* board games and card-based spin-offs, exploring how these games expand the franchise while offering unique gameplay experiences. We'll highlight some of the most popular *Yu-Gi-Oh!* board games, discuss their mechanics, and explain why they make excellent gifts for fans who want to experience the *Yu-Gi-Oh!* universe in a new way.

The Appeal of Yu-Gi-Oh! Themed Board Games

Board games based on the *Yu-Gi-Oh!* universe provide a refreshing way for fans to interact with the characters, duels, and strategies they love, without being bound by the rules of the traditional TCG. These games often feature simplified mechanics, making them accessible to a wider range of players, including those who may not be familiar with the intricacies of the TCG. Additionally, board games offer the opportunity for multiplayer experiences, allowing friends and family to enjoy the game together in a more social setting.

Here's why *Yu-Gi-Oh!* themed board games are so appealing:

1. **Alternative Gameplay**: For fans who may be looking for a break from the competitive nature of the TCG, board games offer a dif-

ferent style of gameplay that's often more casual and suited for group play. These games allow players to enjoy the *Yu-Gi-Oh!* universe in a relaxed setting while still engaging in strategic battles and problem-solving.

2. **Accessible for New Players**: Board games based on *Yu-Gi-Oh!* often have simplified rules compared to the TCG, making them perfect for new players who may be unfamiliar with the more complex mechanics of the card game. This accessibility allows a wider audience, including younger players or those who don't typically play card games, to enjoy the *Yu-Gi-Oh!* experience.

3. **Multiplayer Fun**: Unlike the traditional TCG, which is often limited to two-player duels, *Yu-Gi-Oh!* themed board games often allow for more players, making them great for group gatherings, game nights, or family fun. The social aspect of board games enhances the experience and allows fans to enjoy the *Yu-Gi-Oh!* universe together.

4. **Expanded Storytelling**: Many *Yu-Gi-Oh!* themed board games introduce story elements or scenarios that go beyond the typical dueling experience. These games can offer rich narratives and allow players to interact with the *Yu-Gi-Oh!* world in new and exciting ways, whether by exploring new character dynamics or revisiting iconic battles from the anime.

Popular Yu-Gi-Oh! Themed Board Games

Over the years, Konami and other publishers have released several *Yu-Gi-Oh!* themed board games and spin-offs that offer players unique ways to experience the franchise. These games range from cooperative strategy games to competitive, card-based adventures. Below are some of the most popular and well-received *Yu-Gi-Oh!* themed board games, each offering a distinctive gameplay experience.

1. Yu-Gi-Oh! Monopoly

One of the most iconic board games in the world has been reimagined with *Yu-Gi-Oh!* characters, monsters, and locations. *Yu-Gi-Oh!*

Monopoly brings the classic real estate trading game into the *Yu-Gi-Oh!* universe, where players buy, sell, and trade duel arenas and locations from the anime.

- **Gameplay Overview**: In *Yu-Gi-Oh! Monopoly*, players take on the roles of famous duelists such as *Yugi, Kaiba, Joey,* or *Mai* as they move around the board, purchasing iconic locations like the Duelist Kingdom, Battle City, and Domino High School. Instead of traditional property development, players use their *Yu-Gi-Oh!* monsters and characters to control these areas and collect rent from other players. The game includes themed currency, Chance and Community Chest cards inspired by *Yu-Gi-Oh!*, and custom player tokens shaped like famous monsters such as *Blue-Eyes White Dragon, Dark Magician,* and *Exodia*.
- **Why It's Popular**: *Yu-Gi-Oh! Monopoly* offers a fun twist on a classic game, making it accessible to fans of both *Yu-Gi-Oh!* and traditional board games. The familiarity of the Monopoly mechanics combined with the *Yu-Gi-Oh!* theme makes it a great choice for family game nights or casual play with friends.
- **Ideal For**: Fans of both *Yu-Gi-Oh!* and traditional board games who want to experience the franchise in a fun, competitive, and social setting. *Yu-Gi-Oh! Monopoly* is perfect for casual players and collectors who appreciate the franchise's iconic locations and characters.

2. Yu-Gi-Oh! Dungeon Dice Monsters

Based on the dice-based game featured in the original *Yu-Gi-Oh!* anime, *Dungeon Dice Monsters* offers a completely different take on *Yu-Gi-Oh!* strategy. Rather than using cards to duel, players roll dice to summon monsters and traverse a dungeon-like board to defeat their opponent.

- **Gameplay Overview**: In *Dungeon Dice Monsters*, players compete to reduce their opponent's Life Points to zero by strategically summoning monsters and placing dungeon tiles to navigate the board. Each monster is summoned using a set of special dice, which must be rolled to activate the monster's abilities. As players summon monsters, they place dungeon tiles on the board to form pathways to their opponent. The goal is to destroy the enemy's Dungeon Master (representing the player), while defending your own Dungeon Master with powerful monsters and strategic tile placements.
- **Why It's Popular**: *Dungeon Dice Monsters* is a fan-favorite because it allows players to experience a unique *Yu-Gi-Oh!* duel without relying on traditional cards. The game's dice-based mechanics offer a fresh take on the franchise, introducing more spatial strategy as players place dungeon tiles and monsters to outmaneuver their opponents.
- **Ideal For**: Fans of strategy and board games who enjoy the tactical aspects of *Yu-Gi-Oh!*, but want a new and unique gameplay experience. *Dungeon Dice Monsters* is perfect for players who appreciate puzzle-like mechanics and strategic planning.

3. Yu-Gi-Oh! Millennium Blades

Although *Millennium Blades* is a third-party, *Yu-Gi-Oh!*-inspired board game, it successfully captures the spirit of the *Yu-Gi-Oh!* TCG in a different context. *Millennium Blades* is a game about collecting cards, building decks, and competing in tournaments, all within the meta-world of a fictional trading card game.

- **Gameplay Overview**: In *Millennium Blades*, players take on the roles of professional trading card game players competing in high-stakes tournaments. The game simulates the experience of being part of a TCG community—players buy, sell, and trade cards, build their decks, and participate in tournaments to become the world champion. The game is played over several phases, including a deck-building phase where players manage their resources and a tournament phase where they compete against other players to score victory points.

- **Why It's Popular**: *Millennium Blades* is a unique and meta take on the trading card game experience, allowing players to immerse themselves in a world where deck-building and tournament play are the core elements. The game's clever mechanics, humorous references to card game culture, and competitive edge make it a hit among players who love strategy games and TCGs.
- **Ideal For**: Fans of card games who appreciate the meta aspects of the TCG community. *Millennium Blades* is perfect for players who enjoy deck-building, trading, and competitive strategy, making it a great fit for both *Yu-Gi-Oh!* fans and general card game enthusiasts.

4. Yu-Gi-Oh! Speed Duel Starter Sets and Board Games

The *Yu-Gi-Oh! Speed Duel* format, a simplified version of the traditional TCG, offers fast-paced duels that can be played with starter decks designed for quick, accessible gameplay. While not strictly a board game, *Speed Duel* starter sets are packaged in a way that makes them ideal for casual or group play, similar to board games.

- **Gameplay Overview**: *Speed Duel* simplifies the standard *Yu-Gi-Oh!* TCG rules by reducing the size of the field, limiting deck sizes, and offering quicker games. Starter sets often come with pre-built decks that allow players to jump into a duel without the need for extensive deck-building. Each deck is themed around iconic characters, and the gameplay emphasizes fast, strategic decisions with simplified mechanics.
- **Why It's Popular**: *Speed Duel* is popular because it offers the excitement of *Yu-Gi-Oh!* dueling in a faster and more accessible format. These sets are perfect for quick matches between friends or

as a casual alternative to the more complex TCG format. They're also great for introducing new players to the basics of *Yu-Gi-Oh!*.

- **Ideal For**: Players who enjoy fast-paced, casual gameplay and are looking for an easy way to jump into duels without building complex decks. *Speed Duel* starter sets are also ideal for newcomers to the franchise who want to learn the mechanics of *Yu-Gi-Oh!* in a simpler, more approachable format.

5. Yu-Gi-Oh! Capsule Monsters Coliseum

Although *Capsule Monsters* is primarily known from the anime spin-off arc, there is also a board game version that brings this unique gameplay style into the real world. *Yu-Gi-Oh! Capsule Monsters Coliseum* allows players to summon monsters using capsules and battle them on a grid-based battlefield.

- **Gameplay Overview**: In *Capsule Monsters*, players summon monsters using capsules and move them across a grid to engage in tactical battles. Each monster has its own movement and attack patterns, making positioning and strategy crucial to winning the game. The objective is to defeat the opponent's monsters and reduce their Life Points to zero by using smart positioning and monster abilities.

- **Why It's Popular**: *Capsule Monsters* adds a strategic, chess-like element to the *Yu-Gi-Oh!* universe, where the placement and movement of monsters are just as important as their abilities. Fans of tactical board games will enjoy the challenge of positioning their monsters on the battlefield while considering attack ranges and movement limitations.

- **Ideal For**: Fans of tactical board games and those who enjoy the strategic aspects of *Yu-Gi-Oh!*, but with an added layer of spatial thinking. *Capsule Monsters* is perfect for players who want to experience a different style of dueling that emphasizes battlefield strategy.

Why Yu-Gi-Oh! Themed Board Games Make Excellent Gifts

Yu-Gi-Oh! themed board games offer an alternative way to experience the franchise's beloved characters, monsters, and duels, making them excellent gifts for fans who want to explore new forms of gameplay. Here's why they make such great gifts:

- **Social and Multiplayer Fun**: Unlike the one-on-one nature of the TCG, many *Yu-Gi-Oh!* board games allow for multiple players, making them ideal for family game nights, group gatherings, or parties. These games offer an engaging and social experience that everyone can enjoy.
- **Accessible for All Ages**: Many *Yu-Gi-Oh!* board games have simplified mechanics, making them suitable for players of all ages and skill levels. This accessibility allows fans young and old to enjoy the *Yu-Gi-Oh!* universe without the learning curve of the TCG.
- **Expanded Gameplay Options**: For fans who may have grown tired of the traditional TCG format, board games offer fresh and exciting new ways to engage with the *Yu-Gi-Oh!* world. These games introduce unique mechanics, such as dice-rolling, dungeon-crawling, or grid-based combat, giving players more variety in how they experience the franchise.
- **Great for Collectors**: Many *Yu-Gi-Oh!* themed board games feature beautifully designed components, such as custom dice, detailed figurines, or cards with unique artwork. These elements make the games not only fun to play but also valuable collectibles for fans of the franchise.

Conclusion

Yu-Gi-Oh! themed board games offer a fresh and exciting way to experience the beloved franchise beyond the traditional TCG. Whether it's rolling dice in *Dungeon Dice Monsters*, collecting properties in *Yu-Gi-Oh! Monopoly*, or battling with monsters in *Capsule Monsters*, these games provide fans with unique gameplay experiences that bring the characters, monsters, and strategies of the *Yu-Gi-Oh!* universe to life in new ways. These board games make excellent gifts for fans of all ages and skill levels, offering a fun and social way to enjoy the world of *Yu-Gi-Oh!*.

Chapter 14: Subscription Services for Card Delivery

In recent years, subscription services have become increasingly popular across many hobbies, offering convenience, surprise, and the joy of regular deliveries. For *Yu-Gi-Oh!* fans, card subscription services are an exciting and emerging trend that provides a unique and recurring way to engage with the franchise. These subscription services deliver booster packs, exclusive cards, and other *Yu-Gi-Oh!* merchandise directly to subscribers' doorsteps, offering an ongoing thrill for collectors, players, and enthusiasts. As a gift that keeps giving long after special occasions like Christmas or birthdays, card subscription services offer a monthly dose of excitement and anticipation, making them an ideal choice for any dedicated *Yu-Gi-Oh!* fan.

In this chapter, we'll explore the growing trend of subscription services for *Yu-Gi-Oh!* card deliveries, examine the various types of services available, and explain why they make excellent gifts. We'll also provide recommendations for some of the best subscription boxes on the market and offer tips on how to choose the perfect service based on the recipient's interests, whether they're a casual collector, competitive player, or avid *Yu-Gi-Oh!* fan.

The Appeal of Subscription Services for Yu-Gi-Oh! Fans

The allure of booster packs is undeniable—there's a thrill in opening each pack and the anticipation of discovering rare or powerful cards that could complete a deck or become the highlight of a collection. Subscription services amplify this excitement by delivering new packs, cards, and merchandise on a monthly basis, turning each delivery into a surprise event that keeps the fun of collecting and playing *Yu-Gi-Oh!* alive throughout the year.

Here's why subscription services for *Yu-Gi-Oh!* card deliveries are so appealing:

1. **Ongoing Excitement**: One of the main draws of subscription services is the element of surprise. Each month, subscribers receive a curated selection of booster packs, rare cards, or themed items, keeping the excitement of collecting alive. This regular delivery ensures that fans always have something to look forward to, long after the initial gift is given.

2. **Convenience**: For players and collectors who may not have easy access to card shops or local *Yu-Gi-Oh!* events, subscription services offer a convenient way to receive new cards regularly. There's no need to visit stores or search online for booster packs—subscribers receive the latest releases and exclusive cards directly to their homes.

3. **Exclusive Content**: Many subscription services include exclusive cards, promos, or merchandise that can't be found in regular retail stores. This makes the service particularly attractive to collectors looking for unique or hard-to-find items to add to their collection.

4. **Variety**: Subscription services often include a diverse range of products, from booster packs and single cards to accessories like card sleeves, playmats, and deck boxes. This variety ensures that each delivery offers something new and exciting, catering to both players and collectors alike.

5. **Great for All Skill Levels**: Whether the recipient is a seasoned duelist or a casual collector, card delivery subscription services cater to fans of all skill levels. These services often offer options that are tailored to different types of players, ensuring that every subscriber gets something that fits their interests and level of involvement in the game.

Types of Yu-Gi-Oh! Subscription Services

Subscription services for *Yu-Gi-Oh!* come in various forms, each offering different types of products and experiences. Some services focus on delivering booster packs and cards for competitive play, while others may cater to collectors or offer exclusive merchandise. Below are the main types of subscription services available for *Yu-Gi-Oh!* fans:

1. Booster Pack Subscriptions

Booster pack subscription services are among the most popular options for *Yu-Gi-Oh!* fans. These services deliver a set number of booster packs from recent or upcoming sets each month, providing players with a steady stream of new cards to expand their decks or collections. Depending on the subscription, these packs may include the latest releases, reprints of popular sets, or special promotional packs.

- **What to Expect:**
    - Monthly deliveries of booster packs from current *Yu-Gi-Oh!* sets.
    - Packs may include both recent releases and special promotional sets.
    - Some services offer themed packs, focusing on specific archetypes or types of cards (e.g., Dragon monsters, HERO archetypes).
- **Why It's Popular**: Booster pack subscriptions are ideal for both competitive players and collectors who want to stay up-to-date with new releases without having to purchase packs individually. The element of surprise with each pack keeps the experience exciting, and there's always the chance of pulling rare, ultra-rare, or even secret rare cards.
- **Best For:**
    - Players looking to regularly expand their card collection.
    - Collectors who enjoy the thrill of opening booster packs and discovering new cards.

◦ Fans who want to stay current with the latest *Yu-Gi-Oh!* sets and releases.

2. Themed Card Subscriptions

Themed card subscription services curate their deliveries around specific archetypes, monsters, or themes. These services are perfect for fans who are passionate about a particular type of deck or strategy, as they deliver cards and booster packs that align with those themes. For example, a subscription might focus on delivering cards that support Dragon decks, HERO archetypes, or Spellcaster strategies.

- **What to Expect**:
    - ◦ Monthly deliveries of cards and packs centered around a specific theme, such as a monster type (e.g., Dragon, Spellcaster) or a deck archetype (e.g., HERO, Synchro).
    - ◦ Themed accessories, such as card sleeves or deck boxes, may be included to match the subscription's focus.
    - ◦ Curated card selections designed to enhance specific deck strategies.
- **Why It's Popular**: Themed card subscriptions are perfect for players who have a favorite archetype or strategy and want to receive cards that support and expand that deck. These services offer a personalized touch, as the curation aligns with the subscriber's preferences and playstyle.
- **Best For**:
    - ◦ Players who specialize in a particular deck type or archetype.
    - ◦ Collectors who focus on building themed collections, such as Dragon or Warrior cards.
    - ◦ Fans who appreciate curated content that enhances their specific decks or strategies.

3. Exclusive Promo and Merchandise Subscriptions

For collectors who are more interested in rare or exclusive items, some subscription services focus on delivering promo cards, limited-edition merchandise, and other collectible items. These services often include exclusive cards that are not available in regular booster packs, as well as accessories like card sleeves, playmats, or figurines that feature beloved characters or monsters from the *Yu-Gi-Oh!* universe.

- **What to Expect**:
    - Monthly deliveries of exclusive promo cards, limited-edition merchandise, and themed accessories.
    - Rare or hard-to-find cards that are not available in retail booster packs.
    - Merchandise such as character figurines, deck boxes, playmats, and themed apparel.
- **Why It's Popular**: Collectors who value exclusivity and rarity will appreciate these subscription services, as they offer access to promo cards and merchandise that are difficult to find elsewhere. The inclusion of themed accessories adds extra value for fans who enjoy collecting *Yu-Gi-Oh!* memorabilia in addition to cards.
- **Best For**:
    - Serious collectors who are looking for rare and exclusive cards.
    - Fans who enjoy *Yu-Gi-Oh!* merchandise beyond the cards, such as playmats, figurines, and apparel.
    - Players who want to add rare promo cards to their collection.

4. Tournament and Competitive Play Subscriptions

For competitive players, some subscription services focus on delivering cards and booster packs tailored to the current *Yu-Gi-Oh!* metagame. These subscriptions are curated with competitive play in mind, offering cards that are valuable in tournaments or useful in high-level play. Subscribers often receive the latest meta-relevant cards, along with resources like strategy guides or deck-building tips.

- **What to Expect**:
  - Monthly deliveries of booster packs and single cards that are relevant to the current *Yu-Gi-Oh!* metagame.
  - Strategy guides, deck lists, or tips for competitive play may be included.
  - Access to cards that are essential for building competitive decks.
- **Why It's Popular**: Competitive players benefit from these subscription services as they provide a consistent source of cards that are useful in tournaments. The curated nature of these subscriptions ensures that subscribers receive cards that align with the evolving metagame, giving them an edge in competitive play.
- **Best For**:
  - Competitive players who participate in local or online tournaments.
  - Duelists who want to stay current with the evolving metagame and deck-building trends.
  - Fans who enjoy receiving curated cards that enhance their tournament decks.

Top Subscription Services for Yu-Gi-Oh! Card Delivery

Here are some of the most popular and highly recommended *Yu-Gi-Oh!* card delivery subscription services available today. Each service offers something unique, whether it's booster packs, themed cards, or exclusive promo items, making them excellent gift options for any *Yu-Gi-Oh!* fan.

1. Yu-Gi-Oh! Box Club

The *Yu-Gi-Oh! Box Club* is a popular subscription service that delivers booster packs, promo cards, and exclusive *Yu-Gi-Oh!* merchandise on a monthly basis. Subscribers receive a curated selection of products, including packs from the latest releases, limited-edition cards, and accessories such as card sleeves or deck boxes. The service offers different subscription tiers, allowing fans to choose the option that best fits their needs and budget.

- **Why It's Great**:
    - Offers a mix of booster packs, exclusive promo cards, and themed accessories.
    - Subscribers can choose from multiple subscription tiers, making it accessible for both casual and serious collectors.
    - Includes rare cards and exclusive merchandise, adding extra value to each delivery.

2. Card Crate: Yu-Gi-Oh! Edition

Card Crate is a subscription service that focuses on delivering booster packs and cards for a variety of TCGs, including *Yu-Gi-Oh!*. Each month, subscribers receive a curated selection of packs from recent and upcoming sets, giving them a steady stream of new cards to expand their collection. *Card Crate* offers customization options, allowing subscribers to choose the type of packs they receive based on their preferences (e.g., Dragon-themed, Spellcaster-themed).

- **Why It's Great**:
  - Customizable subscription options tailored to different themes or card types.
  - Regular delivery of booster packs from recent sets, keeping players up-to-date with the latest cards.
  - Ideal for collectors and players looking to expand their decks.

3. TCG Loot: Yu-Gi-Oh! Edition

TCG Loot specializes in delivering rare and exclusive cards, as well as themed *Yu-Gi-Oh!* accessories. Each month, subscribers receive a mix of rare cards, deck-building tools, and collectibles such as playmats or card sleeves. The service focuses on delivering high-quality items that are perfect for both players and collectors who want to enhance their gaming experience.

- **Why It's Great**:
  - Delivers rare and exclusive cards that are hard to find in regular booster packs.
  - Includes premium accessories such as custom playmats, card sleeves, and deck boxes.

    ◦ Ideal for collectors who value unique and high-quality *Yu-Gi-Oh!* merchandise.

How to Choose the Right Subscription Service

When selecting a subscription service for *Yu-Gi-Oh!* card delivery, consider the recipient's preferences and level of involvement in the game. Here are some tips for choosing the perfect service:

1. **For Competitive Players**: Look for a subscription service that focuses on delivering meta-relevant cards and strategy guides. Competitive players will appreciate services that provide cards useful for tournament play.
2. **For Casual Collectors**: Booster pack subscriptions or themed card subscriptions are ideal for collectors who enjoy expanding their collection with a variety of cards. These services offer regular deliveries of new packs, keeping the excitement alive.
3. **For Fans of Exclusive Content**: Choose a subscription service that specializes in delivering rare promo cards, exclusive merchandise, or themed accessories. These services are perfect for fans who love collecting *Yu-Gi-Oh!* memorabilia in addition to cards.
4. **For Younger Fans or Beginners**: Themed card subscriptions or starter deck subscriptions are great for younger fans or newcomers to the franchise. These services often include pre-built decks or easy-to-use cards that help new players learn the game.

Why Subscription Services Make Excellent Gifts

Subscription services for *Yu-Gi-Oh!* card deliveries offer the ultimate gift that keeps on giving. Each month, subscribers receive a new selection of cards, booster packs, and exclusive items, allowing them to continually expand their collection or improve their decks. This ongoing excitement and anticipation make subscription services a standout gift for any *Yu-Gi-Oh!* fan, providing a steady stream of surprises long after the initial gift is given.

- **Lasting Excitement**: The monthly deliveries ensure that the recipient continues to enjoy their gift throughout the year, making it a memorable and long-lasting experience.
- **Tailored to Interests**: With options ranging from booster packs to themed cards and exclusive promo items, subscription services can be tailored to the recipient's specific interests, ensuring they receive products they'll love.
- **Convenient and Accessible**: For fans who may not have easy access to local card shops or events, subscription services provide a convenient way to stay connected to the *Yu-Gi-Oh!* community and receive the latest releases.

Conclusion

Subscription services for *Yu-Gi-Oh!* card deliveries offer fans a thrilling and convenient way to experience the joy of collecting and playing *Yu-Gi-Oh!* all year round. Whether you're gifting a competitive player, a casual collector, or someone who loves exclusive promo cards, these services provide a personalized and ongoing gift that keeps on giving. With a variety of options to choose from—ranging from booster pack subscriptions to themed card deliveries—there's a subscription service that perfectly matches the interests of any *Yu-Gi-Oh!* fan.

Chapter 15: Yu-Gi-Oh! Community Memberships

For devoted *Yu-Gi-Oh!* fans, the game often extends beyond collecting cards and dueling friends—it involves connecting with a passionate community, participating in tournaments, and keeping up with the latest trends in competitive play. If the recipient is already deeply immersed in the *Yu-Gi-Oh!* universe, gifting a community membership, access to tournaments, or gift cards for online *Yu-Gi-Oh!* platforms can significantly enhance their experience. These types of gifts offer a unique opportunity for players to expand their collections, improve their strategies, and become even more engaged with the *Yu-Gi-Oh!* community.

This chapter explores various types of *Yu-Gi-Oh!* community memberships, including online tournament access, premium subscriptions, and gift cards for digital platforms, explaining how each one can enrich a fan's experience. We'll also cover popular online communities, their benefits, and how to choose the right type of membership or digital access based on the recipient's involvement in the game.

The Appeal of Yu-Gi-Oh! Community Memberships

Memberships in online *Yu-Gi-Oh!* communities or tournament access can significantly boost a fan's connection to the game, providing opportunities to engage with like-minded players, improve their deck-building skills, and access exclusive rewards. For players already active in the game, these types of memberships offer an enhanced experience that goes beyond casual play, making them perfect gifts for fans who are ready to dive deeper into the competitive side of the game.

Here's why *Yu-Gi-Oh!* community memberships and digital platform access are appealing:

1. **Competitive Play and Tournaments**: For competitive players, community memberships often grant access to online tournaments, regional qualifiers, and ranked matches. These events provide a thrilling opportunity to test their skills against other top-tier duelists.

2. **Connection with Other Players**: Online *Yu-Gi-Oh!* communities offer a platform where fans can meet other players, share deck strategies, and discuss the latest trends in the metagame. These connections foster a sense of belonging and camaraderie, essential to the enjoyment of competitive and social gaming.

3. **Exclusive Content and Rewards**: Many online communities or premium memberships offer exclusive rewards like digital card packs, strategy guides, early access to new releases, or in-game currency, making the membership even more valuable.

4. **Continual Engagement**: With community memberships, the gift doesn't end with one-time use—it provides ongoing access to resources, events, and competitions throughout the year. This long-term engagement makes it a gift that keeps giving, allowing fans to continuously improve their skills and expand their collections.

5. **Accessibility and Convenience**: With most community memberships available online, players can participate in events and connect with others from anywhere. This accessibility is perfect for fans who want to be part of the broader *Yu-Gi-Oh!* world, even if they can't attend local tournaments.

Types of Yu-Gi-Oh! Community Memberships

Several types of memberships and services are available for *Yu-Gi-Oh!* fans, each catering to different aspects of the game. Whether the recipient is a competitive duelist, a collector, or someone who loves to stay connected with the latest news and strategies, there's a membership that suits their needs.

1. Online Tournament Memberships

For competitive players, gaining access to online tournaments is a key way to test their skills and build their reputation. Many platforms offer tournament memberships that provide exclusive access to ranked matches, regional qualifiers, and even official *Yu-Gi-Oh!* Championship

Series (YCS) events. These memberships allow players to compete at higher levels, earn rewards, and improve their overall performance.

- **What to Expect**:
  - Access to local and regional tournaments, as well as national qualifiers.
  - Opportunities to participate in official *Yu-Gi-Oh!* Remote Duel events hosted by Konami.
  - Online rankings and leaderboards that track progress and help players compete at their best.
  - Exclusive in-game rewards for tournament winners, such as rare cards or in-game currency.
- **Why It's Popular**: For competitive players, the thrill of tournaments is unparalleled. Online tournaments allow duelists to challenge themselves against other skilled players, hone their strategies, and potentially earn recognition in the broader *Yu-Gi-Oh!* community.
- **Best For**:
  - Competitive duelists who want to take their skills to the next level.
  - Players who enjoy participating in regional qualifiers or official *Yu-Gi-Oh!* tournaments.
  - Fans who thrive in competitive environments and enjoy testing their decks in real-time against other skilled players.

2. Subscription Services for Digital Yu-Gi-Oh! Platforms

With digital platforms like *Yu-Gi-Oh! Master Duel* and *Yu-Gi-Oh! Duel Links* becoming increasingly popular, many fans engage in the *Yu-Gi-Oh!* world online. These platforms often offer premium subscription services that give players access to exclusive content, in-game rewards, and ranked duels. Subscriptions provide ongoing access to card packs, special events, and high-level strategies that help players stay ahead of the competition.

- **What to Expect**:
    - Monthly or annual subscriptions to digital platforms such as *Master Duel* or *Duel Links*.
    - Exclusive digital card packs, in-game currency, and cosmetic upgrades like sleeves and playmats.
    - Access to ranked duels, special events, and regular updates that keep the game fresh and engaging.
    - Premium resources such as strategy guides, deck-building tools, and early access to new card sets.
- **Why It's Popular**: For fans who enjoy playing *Yu-Gi-Oh!* online, subscription services provide continuous engagement with the game. These services give players access to exclusive content and in-game items that help them expand their digital card collections and compete in online duels.
- **Best For**:
    - Fans of *Yu-Gi-Oh! Master Duel* or *Duel Links* who want to maximize their in-game experience.
    - Players who enjoy ranked duels and special online events.
    - Duelists who appreciate the convenience of digital card collecting and competitive play.

3. Memberships to Yu-Gi-Oh! Strategy Communities

For players who are serious about improving their skills, memberships to strategy-based communities are a valuable gift. These communities provide in-depth resources like deck lists, tournament-winning strategies, card analysis, and metagame discussions that help players refine their decks and stay up-to-date with the latest developments in the game.

- **What to Expect**:
    - Access to exclusive strategy guides, deck lists, and in-depth card analysis.

- ° Discussion forums where players can connect with high-level duelists, share insights, and ask for advice.
- ° Regular updates on new card releases, rules changes, and trends in the *Yu-Gi-Oh!* metagame.
- ° Advanced tools for deck-building, including databases of top-performing cards and strategies.
- **Why It's Popular**: Competitive players value strategy communities because they provide insights that can give them an edge in tournaments and ranked matches. These communities offer a wealth of knowledge, making them an essential resource for anyone looking to improve their gameplay.
- **Best For**:
  - ° Serious players who want to refine their strategies and deck-building skills.
  - ° Fans who enjoy staying on top of the latest developments in the *Yu-Gi-Oh!* metagame.
  - ° Duelists who appreciate being part of a community where they can discuss tactics and share ideas with others.

4. Gift Cards for Yu-Gi-Oh! Digital Platforms

If you're unsure which membership or platform is best for the recipient, gift cards for *Yu-Gi-Oh!* digital platforms offer a flexible option. Many platforms, such as *Yu-Gi-Oh! Master Duel*, *Duel Links*, and *TCG-Player*, allow players to purchase in-game currency, card packs, or premium content using gift cards. This gives the recipient the freedom to choose the cards or items they want, allowing them to tailor the experience to their specific needs.

- **What to Expect**:
  - ° Gift cards or digital credits that can be redeemed for in-game currency, card packs, or premium content on popular *Yu-Gi-Oh!* platforms.

- ◦ Flexibility to use the gift card for digital cards, deck-building tools, or cosmetic upgrades like card sleeves and avatars.
  - ◦ Can be used on platforms like *Master Duel*, *Duel Links*, or TCGPlayer to enhance the recipient's card collection or competitive play.
- **Why It's Popular**: Gift cards offer the perfect solution when you want to give the recipient the freedom to choose their own in-game purchases. This flexibility makes it easy for players to expand their collections, build new decks, or participate in exclusive events.
- **Best For**:
  - ◦ Fans who enjoy playing *Yu-Gi-Oh!* on digital platforms and want the flexibility to customize their experience.
  - ◦ Players who enjoy purchasing booster packs, card packs, or in-game items to enhance their decks.
  - ◦ Duelists who appreciate the option to use gift cards across various *Yu-Gi-Oh!* digital platforms.

5. Official Yu-Gi-Oh! Remote Duel Events Memberships

The *Yu-Gi-Oh!* Remote Duel system allows players to participate in official tournaments and events from the comfort of their homes. Memberships or passes for Remote Duel events provide access to official Konami tournaments, regional qualifiers, and even the *Yu-Gi-Oh!* Championship Series (YCS). These events allow players to compete at the highest level without needing to attend in-person events.

- **What to Expect**:
  - ◦ Access to official Remote Duel tournaments and regional qualifiers.
  - ◦ Participation in the *Yu-Gi-Oh!* Championship Series (YCS) through remote play.
  - ◦ Opportunities to compete for prizes, recognition, and qualification for higher-level tournaments.

- Memberships often include entry fees for events and access to exclusive rewards or digital content.
- **Why It's Popular**: Remote Duel events have become increasingly popular as they offer a convenient way for players to compete in official tournaments without needing to travel. For serious players, these events provide an excellent opportunity to showcase their skills and gain recognition in the community.
- **Best For**:
    - Competitive duelists who want to participate in official *Yu-Gi-Oh!* events and tournaments.
    - Players who enjoy high-level competitive play and want the convenience of participating from home.
    - Fans who aim to qualify for regional or national-level *Yu-Gi-Oh!* tournaments.

Why Yu-Gi-Oh! Community Memberships Make Excellent Gifts

For experienced *Yu-Gi-Oh!* players, community memberships and access to tournaments or digital platforms provide an exciting and valuable way to deepen their involvement in the game. Whether through exclusive access to competitive play, premium content, or strategy resources, these memberships enhance the player's experience and help them stay connected with the broader *Yu-Gi-Oh!* community.

Here's why community memberships make excellent gifts:

- **Ongoing Value**: Unlike one-time gifts, community memberships offer continuous access to tournaments, exclusive content, and resources, making them a gift that provides value throughout the year.
- **Enhanced Gameplay**: For competitive players, memberships provide opportunities to improve their skills, access exclusive content, and participate in high-level tournaments, elevating their gameplay experience.

- **Connection to the Community**: Being part of an active *Yu-Gi-Oh!* community allows players to connect with like-minded duelists, share strategies, and form friendships, making the game even more enjoyable.
- **Flexible Options**: Whether through tournament memberships, strategy guides, or gift cards, there are various ways to tailor a membership or access service to the recipient's interests and level of involvement in the game.

Conclusion

Yu-Gi-Oh! community memberships, tournament access, and digital platform subscriptions provide a unique and valuable way for fans to enhance their involvement in the game. Whether the recipient is a competitive player looking to test their skills in tournaments or a fan who loves connecting with others in the *Yu-Gi-Oh!* community, these memberships offer ongoing benefits that enrich their experience. With options ranging from online tournaments to premium digital content, you can find the perfect membership or service to suit the recipient's needs, making it a thoughtful and engaging gift for any *Yu-Gi-Oh!* fan.

Chapter 16: Holiday-Themed Yu-Gi-Oh! Gifts

The holiday season is a time of joy, celebration, and gift-giving, and for *Yu-Gi-Oh!* fans, the perfect gift can make the season even more magical. Whether the recipient is a casual player or a dedicated collector, there are endless opportunities to get creative with holiday-themed *Yu-Gi-Oh!* gifts that capture the spirit of the season. From limited-edition holiday card sets and decorations to fun stocking stuffers and themed accessories, *Yu-Gi-Oh!* fans of all ages will love unwrapping presents that celebrate their favorite franchise in festive ways.

In this final chapter, we'll explore creative and exciting ideas for holiday-themed *Yu-Gi-Oh!* gifts, offering suggestions for gifts that combine the magic of the holiday season with the excitement of the *Yu-Gi-Oh!* universe. We'll also provide guidance on how to create the ultimate gift bundle that includes everything from community memberships and subscription services to apparel and stocking stuffers, ensuring that the *Yu-Gi-Oh!* fan in your life has a holiday they'll never forget.

The Appeal of Holiday-Themed Yu-Gi-Oh! Gifts

Holiday-themed *Yu-Gi-Oh!* gifts are a fun and festive way to celebrate the season with something that resonates with the recipient's passion for the game. Whether it's a special-edition holiday card set or *Yu-Gi-Oh!* decorations for the tree, these gifts offer a unique way to blend the excitement of the holidays with the thrill of the *Yu-Gi-Oh!* universe. Plus, holiday-themed gifts often come with exclusive or limited-edition items that can't be found at other times of the year, making them even more special.

Here's why holiday-themed *Yu-Gi-Oh!* gifts are so appealing:

1. **Exclusive Holiday Items**: Many *Yu-Gi-Oh!* products released during the holiday season feature limited-edition cards, themed merchandise, or collectible items that are only available during

this time of year. These exclusive items are highly sought after by fans and make for memorable gifts.

2. **Festive Fun**: Holiday-themed gifts allow fans to celebrate their love for *Yu-Gi-Oh!* in a festive and creative way. Whether it's decorations, holiday card sets, or themed accessories, these gifts help bring the spirit of the season to life for fans of all ages.

3. **Perfect for Collectors**: For collectors, holiday gifts often include rare or unique items that can't be found elsewhere. Special-edition holiday cards, ornaments, or figurines are perfect for adding to a fan's collection, making them valuable keepsakes.

4. **Fun for All Ages**: From stocking stuffers to elaborate gift bundles, holiday-themed *Yu-Gi-Oh!* gifts cater to fans of all ages, making them a great way to spread holiday cheer among younger fans as well as adult collectors and players.

Creative Ideas for Holiday-Themed Yu-Gi-Oh! Gifts

When it comes to holiday gift-giving, there are countless ways to incorporate the *Yu-Gi-Oh!* franchise into your presents. Whether it's through limited-edition holiday card sets, collectible ornaments, or themed accessories, these gifts are sure to bring joy to any fan. Below are some of the most creative ideas for *Yu-Gi-Oh!* holiday-themed gifts.

1. Yu-Gi-Oh! Holiday Card Sets

One of the most exciting gifts for any *Yu-Gi-Oh!* fan is a holiday-themed card set. Some sets are specifically designed for the holiday season, featuring exclusive cards with festive designs or limited-edition artwork. These sets often come packaged in holiday-themed boxes or tins, making them perfect for gifting.

- **What to Expect**:
  - Special-edition holiday card sets featuring exclusive artwork, such as *Yu-Gi-Oh!* monsters in festive settings or wearing holiday attire.

- ◦ Packs that include rare or ultra-rare cards, often with limited availability during the holiday season.
- ◦ Themed packaging, such as holiday-themed tins or collectible boxes, making the gift extra special.
- **Popular Holiday Card Sets**:
  - ◦ **Holiday Tin Sets**: These tins often feature exclusive cards with holiday-themed designs or limited-edition reprints of popular cards. They make for a great collectible item that fans can cherish long after the holiday season.
  - ◦ **Christmas-Themed Booster Packs**: Some companies release holiday-themed booster packs that include cards with festive designs or special holiday symbols. These packs offer a fun twist on traditional *Yu-Gi-Oh!* cards and make for a great gift.
- **Why It's Popular**: Holiday card sets are perfect for collectors and players alike, offering exclusive cards and festive packaging that make them a great keepsake. The excitement of opening a special holiday-themed set is a gift that any fan will appreciate.

2. Yu-Gi-Oh! Decorations and Ornaments

Decorating the home or tree with *Yu-Gi-Oh!* ornaments and decorations is a fun way for fans to celebrate their love for the franchise during the holidays. From collectible ornaments featuring popular monsters to *Yu-Gi-Oh!*-themed holiday lights, there are plenty of festive decorations that make for unique and thoughtful gifts.

- **What to Expect**:
  - ◦ Holiday ornaments featuring iconic *Yu-Gi-Oh!* monsters, such as *Dark Magician*, *Blue-Eyes White Dragon*, or *Red-Eyes Black Dragon*, in festive poses.
  - ◦ *Yu-Gi-Oh!* holiday lights or garlands featuring card-themed designs or favorite characters.

- Holiday stockings or tree skirts with *Yu-Gi-Oh!* logos or character designs, perfect for adding a bit of fandom flair to holiday decor.
- **Popular Holiday Decorations**:
  - **Character Ornaments**: Many companies produce ornaments featuring *Yu-Gi-Oh!* characters or monsters, making them perfect for hanging on the tree or displaying during the holiday season. For example, ornaments featuring *Yugi*, *Kaiba*, or *Dark Magician Girl* are popular choices for fans of the original series.
  - **Holiday Stockings**: Custom *Yu-Gi-Oh!* stockings make great gifts and can be personalized with the recipient's favorite character or monster. These are perfect for filling with smaller *Yu-Gi-Oh!* gifts like booster packs or card sleeves.
- **Why It's Popular**: *Yu-Gi-Oh!* decorations allow fans to blend their passion for the game with holiday traditions, making these items perfect for fans who love decorating their homes or trees with festive and fandom-inspired pieces.

3. Yu-Gi-Oh! Themed Stocking Stuffers

Stocking stuffers are a fun and easy way to fill a *Yu-Gi-Oh!* fan's holiday stocking with surprises that celebrate their love for the game. From small accessories and card sleeves to collectible mini-figures and booster packs, there's a wide range of *Yu-Gi-Oh!* items that make perfect stocking stuffers.

- **What to Expect**:
  - Small booster packs, promo cards, or single-card sleeves featuring popular *Yu-Gi-Oh!* characters or monsters.
  - *Yu-Gi-Oh!* accessories, such as keychains, pins, or lanyards with character designs or iconic symbols like the *Millennium Puzzle*.

- Collectible mini-figures of *Yu-Gi-Oh!* monsters or duelists, ideal for displaying or adding to a collection.
- **Popular Stocking Stuffer Ideas**:
  - **Booster Packs**: A few packs from the latest *Yu-Gi-Oh!* set make a great stocking stuffer, allowing fans to expand their collections or build new decks.
  - **Card Sleeves**: Themed card sleeves featuring characters or monsters like *Yugi* or *Kaiba* are practical and make for an excellent small gift.
  - **Mini-Figures**: Collectible mini-figures of popular characters and monsters can be found in blind bags or small packs, adding an element of surprise to each stocking stuffer.
- **Why It's Popular**: Stocking stuffers allow for a variety of small gifts that fans will enjoy unwrapping. These items are fun, affordable, and perfect for younger fans or casual players who appreciate receiving smaller *Yu-Gi-Oh!* surprises during the holidays.

4. Yu-Gi-Oh! Apparel for the Holidays

For fans who enjoy wearing their *Yu-Gi-Oh!* pride, holiday-themed apparel is a fun and stylish way to celebrate the season. From festive sweaters and socks to *Yu-Gi-Oh!*-themed scarves and hats, there are plenty of clothing options that blend fandom with holiday cheer.

- **What to Expect**:
  - Holiday sweaters featuring festive *Yu-Gi-Oh!* designs, such as *Dark Magician* or *Blue-Eyes White Dragon* in winter scenes or wearing Santa hats.
  - Warm *Yu-Gi-Oh!* socks, scarves, or hats featuring popular characters or card symbols.
  - T-shirts or hoodies with holiday-themed artwork, perfect for fans who want to showcase their love for the game during the winter months.

- **Popular Holiday Apparel**:
  - ◦ **Ugly Christmas Sweaters**: Ugly holiday sweaters are a fun and lighthearted gift, and *Yu-Gi-Oh!* designs make them even better for fans. Sweaters featuring *Yugi* and his iconic monsters in festive poses are always a hit.
  - ◦ **Holiday Socks**: Cozy socks with *Yu-Gi-Oh!* designs make a great small gift or stocking stuffer. Designs featuring duel monsters in winter scenes or iconic symbols like the *Millennium Puzzle* are perfect for fans who want a subtle yet festive way to show off their fandom.
- **Why It's Popular**: *Yu-Gi-Oh!* holiday apparel is not only practical for the colder months, but it also provides fans with a festive way to showcase their love for the franchise. From cozy socks to fun holiday sweaters, these items are perfect for fans who enjoy adding a little bit of *Yu-Gi-Oh!* flair to their winter wardrobe.

5. Creating the Ultimate Yu-Gi-Oh! Holiday Gift Bundle

For those looking to go all out this holiday season, combining several *Yu-Gi-Oh!* items into a gift bundle creates an unforgettable present that any fan will love. By mixing together community memberships, apparel, subscription services, and themed accessories, you can create a personalized and exciting gift package that provides everything a *Yu-Gi-Oh!* enthusiast could want.

Here's how to build the perfect *Yu-Gi-Oh!* gift bundle:

1. **Start with a Key Gift**: Choose a standout item, such as a special holiday card set, a collector's box, or a tournament membership, to serve as the main centerpiece of the gift. This will be the highlight of the bundle.
2. **Add Stocking Stuffers**: Include smaller items like booster packs, mini-figures, or card sleeves that complement the main gift. These fun extras enhance the gift and make it feel even more special.

3. **Incorporate Apparel or Accessories**: Add in some *Yu-Gi-Oh!* holiday apparel, such as socks, scarves, or a festive t-shirt, to make the bundle feel even more personalized. Apparel adds a practical and stylish touch to the overall package.

4. **Top It Off with a Membership or Subscription**: Include a membership to an online *Yu-Gi-Oh!* community or a subscription service that delivers monthly booster packs or exclusive cards. This ongoing element keeps the excitement going long after the holiday season.

5. **Presentation Matters**: Pack the bundle in a holiday-themed *Yu-Gi-Oh!* tin or collectible box, or wrap it in festive paper featuring the recipient's favorite *Yu-Gi-Oh!* characters. Thoughtful presentation makes the gift even more exciting to unwrap.

- **Why It's Popular**: A *Yu-Gi-Oh!* gift bundle provides the ultimate experience for fans, combining multiple elements that reflect their passion for the game. Whether it's playing in tournaments, expanding their card collection, or showing off their favorite characters through apparel, the bundle creates a memorable and personalized holiday experience.

Conclusion

Holiday-themed *Yu-Gi-Oh!* gifts offer a unique and festive way to celebrate the season while indulging a fan's love for the franchise. Whether it's through special-edition card sets, decorations, apparel, or creative stocking stuffers, these gifts are sure to bring joy to any *Yu-Gi-Oh!* enthusiast. For those looking to go above and beyond, creating a personalized gift bundle that combines holiday-themed items with community memberships and subscriptions ensures that the recipient will have a holiday season filled with *Yu-Gi-Oh!* excitement.

No matter the occasion, whether it's Christmas, a birthday, or another special event, putting thought into a customized *Yu-Gi-Oh!* gift package is the perfect way to show your appreciation for the duelist in your life. With these ideas, you'll be able to craft a memorable and personalized gift that will delight any *Yu-Gi-Oh!* fan, making their holiday season one to remember.

Appendix: Resources and Glossary

This appendix serves as a comprehensive resource for both seasoned *Yu-Gi-Oh!* enthusiasts and those new to the game, helping you find the perfect gift this holiday season. Whether you're searching for the best online platforms to buy *Yu-Gi-Oh!* gifts or trying to understand some of the key terms used in the game, this guide will provide valuable information.

We've compiled a list of recommended websites, stores, and platforms where you can find everything from collectible cards and accessories to board games and apparel. Additionally, we've included a glossary of *Yu-Gi-Oh!* terms to help those unfamiliar with the game better understand its mechanics and terminology.

Section 1: Recommended Websites, Stores, and Platforms

Here are some of the top resources for finding *Yu-Gi-Oh!* gifts, including both online stores and platforms where fans can purchase cards, accessories, and more.

1. Official Yu-Gi-Oh! Store

Website: store.yugioh-card.com

The official *Yu-Gi-Oh!* store offers a wide range of products, including the latest booster packs, tins, structure decks, and exclusive merchandise. This is the go-to source for official, high-quality *Yu-Gi-Oh!* items, perfect for fans of all levels.

Why Shop Here:

- Officially licensed products
- Access to new card releases, bundles, and special collections
- Exclusive merchandise such as playmats, card sleeves, and deck boxes

2. TCGPlayer

Website: www.tcgplayer.com

TCGPlayer is one of the largest online platforms for purchasing trading cards. It offers a massive selection of *Yu-Gi-Oh!* cards, from booster packs and single cards to card sleeves and protective cases. Players can also find rare and hard-to-find cards here.

Why Shop Here:

- Large selection of single cards, booster packs, and accessories
- Competitive pricing and customer reviews
- A marketplace where multiple sellers offer different prices, ensuring variety and availability

3. CardMarket

Website: www.cardmarket.com

CardMarket is Europe's largest marketplace for trading card games, including *Yu-Gi-Oh!*. It allows users to buy and sell cards, accessories, and collectible items. It's particularly useful for fans in Europe, offering a wide range of products and shipping options.

Why Shop Here:

- Ideal for European customers
- A marketplace for new, rare, and used cards
- Competitive pricing and transparent seller ratings

4. eBay

Website: www.ebay.com

eBay is a great platform for finding rare, collectible, or vintage *Yu-Gi-Oh!* cards and merchandise. Many sellers offer unique items, such as promo cards, signed memorabilia, and retired decks, making it an excellent option for collectors.

Why Shop Here:

- Large selection of rare and collectible *Yu-Gi-Oh!* items
- Great for finding older or discontinued cards and sets
- Ability to compare prices and find deals from various sellers

5. Amazon

Website: www.amazon.com

Amazon offers a variety of *Yu-Gi-Oh!* products, from booster packs and collector's tins to apparel and accessories. It's an easy-to-use platform with fast shipping and customer reviews, making it a reliable option for those looking for quick and efficient shopping.

Why Shop Here:

- Wide selection of products, including card sets, apparel, and gifts
- Prime shipping for fast delivery
- Customer reviews for reliable purchasing decisions

6. Hot Topic

Website: www.hottopic.com

Hot Topic is well-known for its pop culture-themed apparel and merchandise, including *Yu-Gi-Oh!* clothing and accessories. They offer unique items such as t-shirts, hoodies, and collectibles that appeal to fans of all ages.

Why Shop Here:

- A variety of *Yu-Gi-Oh!* themed apparel and accessories
- Perfect for fans who love to wear their fandom
- Frequent promotions and discounts

7. Etsy

Website: www.etsy.com

Etsy is a fantastic platform for finding handmade and custom *Yu-Gi-Oh!* items, including custom cards, fan art, and personalized accessories. Many independent sellers create unique gifts, such as custom deck boxes, playmats, and art prints that aren't available anywhere else.

Why Shop Here:

- Handmade, unique, and customizable *Yu-Gi-Oh!* products

- Support independent artists and creators
- Ideal for one-of-a-kind or personalized gifts

8. Target & Walmart

Websites: www.target.com | www.walmart.com

Both Target and Walmart carry a selection of *Yu-Gi-Oh!* products, including booster packs, structure decks, and accessories. While the selection may not be as extensive as specialized stores, these retailers are convenient for shoppers looking for general *Yu-Gi-Oh!* products.

Why Shop Here:

- Convenient in-store and online shopping
- Frequent promotions and sales
- Great for last-minute gift shopping

9. Yu-Gi-Oh! Master Duel and Duel Links (Digital Platforms)

Website: www.masterduel-yugioh.com

Website: www.duellinks.konami.net

Yu-Gi-Oh! Master Duel and *Yu-Gi-Oh! Duel Links* are digital platforms where fans can play *Yu-Gi-Oh!* online. Both platforms offer in-game purchases, allowing players to buy card packs, decks, and other accessories. These platforms also hold regular events and tournaments, making them a great option for fans who enjoy competitive play.

Why Shop Here:

- In-game purchases of digital cards, booster packs, and event tickets
- Access to ranked duels and special events
- Perfect for players who enjoy the digital *Yu-Gi-Oh!* experience

Section 2: Glossary of Yu-Gi-Oh! Terms

For those new to *Yu-Gi-Oh!*, understanding the game's terminology can help in selecting the right gifts and deepening your appreciation of the game. Below is a glossary of common *Yu-Gi-Oh!* terms that will help you navigate the world of dueling and collecting.

Booster Pack

A set of random cards that can be purchased and opened to expand a player's collection. Booster packs typically contain a mix of common, rare, and sometimes ultra-rare or secret-rare cards.

Deck

A set of 40-60 cards that a player builds to duel with. Players create their decks based on their preferred strategies, using monsters, spells, and trap cards.

Duel Disk

A wearable device from the anime that characters use to hold their cards during duels. While primarily a part of the show, toy versions are available for fans who want to recreate the experience.

Fusion Summon

A type of summoning mechanic that allows a player to summon a monster by combining two or more monsters using a *Polymerization* spell card or similar effect. Fusion Monsters are placed in the Extra Deck.

Link Summon

A special summoning mechanic where players use Link Monsters, found in the Extra Deck. These monsters have a "Link Rating" and can be summoned by using the number of monsters that match the rating.

Pendulum Summon

A summoning method that uses Pendulum Monsters placed in the Pendulum Zones. This mechanic allows players to summon multiple monsters at once, creating a strategic advantage.

XYZ Summon

A summoning method that allows players to summon XYZ monsters from the Extra Deck by overlaying monsters of the same level. XYZ monsters are powerful and often have unique abilities.

Synchro Summon

A special summoning method that requires the player to combine a Tuner monster and one or more non-Tuner monsters whose levels add up to the level of the Synchro Monster they wish to summon.

Field Spell

A type of spell card that remains on the field once activated. Field Spells often have lasting effects that benefit one or both players and may impact the overall strategy of the game.

Millennium Items

Magical artifacts from the *Yu-Gi-Oh!* anime that hold great power. Items such as the *Millennium Puzzle* and *Millennium Rod* play crucial roles in the storyline and are frequently depicted on merchandise.

Side Deck

A set of up to 15 cards that a player can swap into their main deck between matches in a best-of-three duel. The Side Deck allows players to adjust their strategy based on their opponent's deck.

Structure Deck

A pre-built deck designed to introduce players to specific strategies or themes. Structure decks are great for beginners or those looking to explore new archetypes without building a deck from scratch.

Extra Deck

The part of a player's deck that holds special monsters such as Fusion, Synchro, XYZ, and Link Monsters. These monsters cannot be drawn during regular gameplay but are summoned through special mechanics.

Archetype

A group of cards that share a theme or naming convention. Archetypes often have synergistic effects that work well when played together.

Examples include *Dark Magician* cards, *HERO* monsters, and *Dragon-maid* cards.

Life Points

The points a player starts with in a duel. A player typically begins with 8000 Life Points, and the goal is to reduce the opponent's Life Points to zero to win the game.

Meta

Refers to the most competitive and frequently used cards, strategies, or decks at a given time. Staying "meta" means using strategies that are proven to be effective in competitive play.

Trap Card

A type of card that can be activated during either player's turn, usually in response to an action taken by the opponent. Trap cards can be used to negate effects, destroy monsters, or alter the course of the duel.

Spell Card

Cards that can be activated during the player's turn, providing effects that range from drawing extra cards to destroying the opponent's monsters or spells. Spell cards are an essential component of any deck.

Conclusion

This appendix has provided a detailed overview of where to find the best *Yu-Gi-Oh!* gifts and a glossary to help navigate the terminology of the game. Whether you're a long-time fan or new to the franchise, this guide will help you select the perfect *Yu-Gi-Oh!* gift this holiday season, ensuring that you find something special for any duelist in your life.

<u>Message from the Author:</u>

I hope you enjoyed this book, I love astrology and knew there was not a book such as this out on the shelf. I love metaphysical items as well. Please check out my other books:

-Life of Government Benefits

-My life of Hell

-My life with Hydrocephalus

-Red Sky

-World Domination:Woman's rule

-World Domination:Woman's Rule 2: The War

-Life and Banishment of Apophis: book 1

-The Kidney Friendly Diet

-The Ultimate Hemp Cookbook

-Creating a Dispensary(legally)

-Cleanliness throughout life: the importance of showering from childhood to adulthood.

-Strong Roots: The Risks of Overcoddling children

-Hemp Horoscopes: Cosmic Insights and Earthly Healing

- Celestial Hemp Navigating the Zodiac: Through the Green Cosmos

-Astrological Hemp: Aligning The Stars with Earth's Ancient Herb

-The Astrological Guide to Hemp: Stars, Signs, and Sacred Leaves

-Green Growth: Innovative Marketing Strategies for your Hemp Products and Dispensary

-Cosmic Cannabis

-Astrological Munchies

-Henry The Hemp

-Zodiacal Roots: The Astrological Soul Of Hemp

- **Green Constellations: Intersection of Hemp and Zodiac**

-Hemp in The Houses: An astrological Adventure Through The Cannabis Galaxy

-Galactic Ganja Guide

Heavenly Hemp

Zodiac Leaves

Doctor Who Astrology

Cannastrology

Stellar Satvias and Cosmic Indicas

Celestial Cannabis: A Zodiac Journey

AstroHerbology: The Sky and The Soil: Volume 1

AstroHerbology:Celestial Cannabis:Volume 2

Cosmic Cannabis Cultivation

The Starry Guide to Herbal Harmony: Volume 1

The Starry Guide to Herbal Harmony: Cannabis Universe: Volume 2

Yugioh Astrology: Astrological Guide to Deck, Duels and more

Nightmare Mansion: Echoes of The Abyss

Nightmare Mansion 2: Legacy of Shadows

Nightmare Mansion 3: Shadows of the Forgotten

Nightmare Mansion 4: Echoes of the Damned

The Life and Banishment of Apophis: Book 2

Nightmare Mansion: Halls of Despair

Healing with Herb: Cannabis and Hydrocephalus

Planetary Pot: Aligning with Astrological Herbs: Volume 1

Fast Track to Freedom: 30 Days to Financial Independence Using AI, Assets, and Agile Hustles

Cosmic Hemp Pathways

How to Become Financially Free in 30 Days: 10,000 Paths to Prosperity

Zodiacal Herbage: Astrological Insights: Volume 1

Nightmare Mansion: Whispers in the Walls

The Daleks Invade Atlantis

Henry the hemp and Hydrocephalus

10X The Kidney Friendly Diet

Cannabis Universe: Adult coloring book

Hemp Astrology: The Healing Power of the Stars

Zodiacal Herbage: Astrological Insights: Cannabis Universe: Volume 2

<u>Planetary Pot: Aligning with Astrological Herbs: Cannabis Universes: Volume 2</u>

Doctor Who Meets the Replicators and SG-1: The Ultimate Battle for Survival

Nightmare Mansion: Curse of the Blood Moon

<u>The Celestial Stoner: A Guide to the Zodiac</u>

Cosmic Pleasures: Sex Toy Astrology for Every Sign

Hydrocephalus Astrology: Navigating the Stars and Healing Waters

Lapis and the Mischievous Chocolate Bar

Celestial Positions: Sexual Astrology for Every Sign

Apophis's Shadow Work Journal: : A Journey of Self-Discovery and Healing

Kinky Cosmos: Sexual Kink Astrology for Every Sign

Digital Cosmos: The Astrological Digimon Compendium

Stellar Seeds: The Cosmic Guide to Growing with Astrology

Apophis's Daily Gratitude Journal

Cat Astrology: Feline Mysteries of the Cosmos

The Cosmic Kama Sutra: An Astrological Guide to Sexual Positions

Unleash Your Potential: A Guided Journal Powered by AI Insights

Whispers of the Enchanted Grove

Cosmic Pleasures: An Astrological Guide to Sexual Kinks

369, 12 Manifestation Journal

Whisper of the nocturne journal(blank journal for writing or drawing)

The Boogey Book

Locked In Reflection: A Chastity Journey Through Locktober

Generating Wealth Quickly:

How to Generate $100,000 in 24 Hours

Star Magic: Harness the Power of the Universe

The Flatulence Chronicles: A Fart Journal for Self-Discovery

The Doctor and The Death Moth

Seize the Day: A Personal Seizure Tracking Journal

The Ultimate Boogeyman Safari: A Journey into the Boogie World and Beyond

Whispers of Samhain: 1,000 Spells of Love, Luck, and Lunar Magic: Samhain Spell Book

Apophis's guides:

Witch's Spellbook Crafting Guide for Halloween

<u>Frost & Flame: The Enchanted Yule Grimoire of 1000 Winter Spells</u>

<u>The Ultimate Boogey Goo Guide & Spooky Activities for Halloween Fun</u>

Harmony of the Scales: A Libra's Spellcraft for Balance and Beauty

The Enchanted Advent: 36 Days of Christmas Wonders

Nightmare Mansion: The Labyrinth of Screams

Harvest of Enchantment: 1,000 Spells of Gratitude, Love, and Fortune for Thanksgiving

The Boogey Chronicles: A Journal of Nightly Encounters and Shadowy Secrets

The 12 Days of Financial Freedom: A Step-by-Step Christmas Countdown to Transform Your Finances

Sigil of the Eternal Spiral Blank Journal

A Christmas Feast: Timeless Recipes for Every Meal

Holiday Stress-Free Solutions: A Survival Guide to Thriving During the Festive Season

If you want solar for your home go here: https://www.harborsolar.live/apophisenterprises/

Get Some Tarot cards: https://www.makeplayingcards.com/sell/apophis-occult-shop

Get some shirts: https://www.bonfire.com/store/apophis-shirt-emporium/

<u>Instagrams:</u>
@apophis_enterprises,
@apophisbookemporium,
@apophisscardshop
Twitter: @apophisenterpr1
Tiktok:@apophisenterprise
Youtube: @sg1fan23477, @FiresideRetreatKingdom
Hive: @sg1fan23477
Podcast: Apophis Chat Zone: https://open.spotify.com/show/
5zXbrCLEV2xzCp8ybrfHsk?si=fb4d4fdbdce44dec

Newsletter: https://apophiss-newsletter-27c897.beehiiv.com/

Get printable holiday budget planners: apophisenterprises-llc.org/Apophis-emporium-shop /ols/products/holiday-budgeting-packageprintable